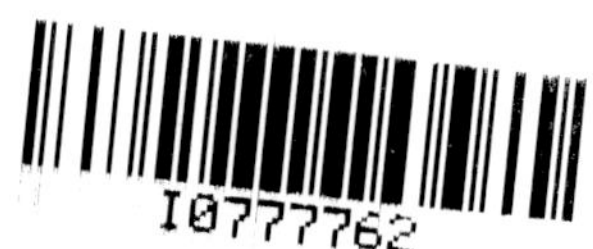

THIS BOOK BELONGS TO

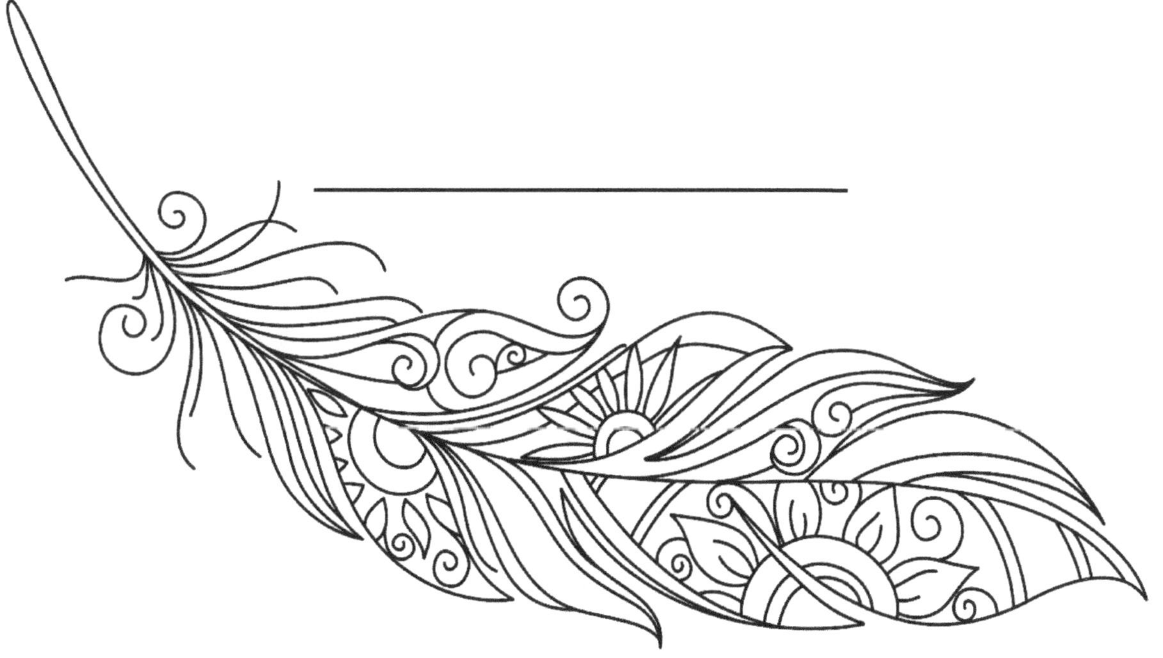

____

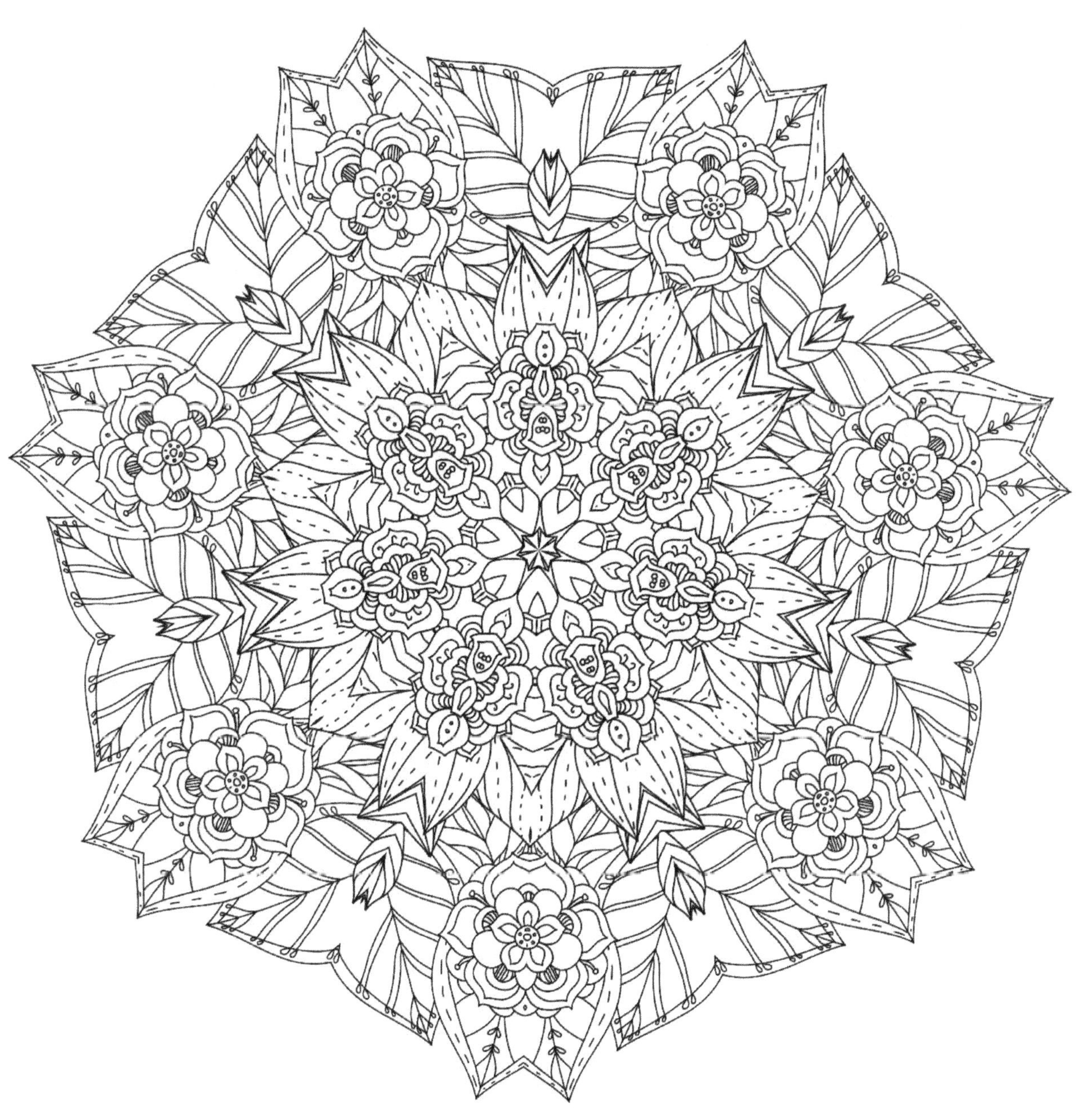

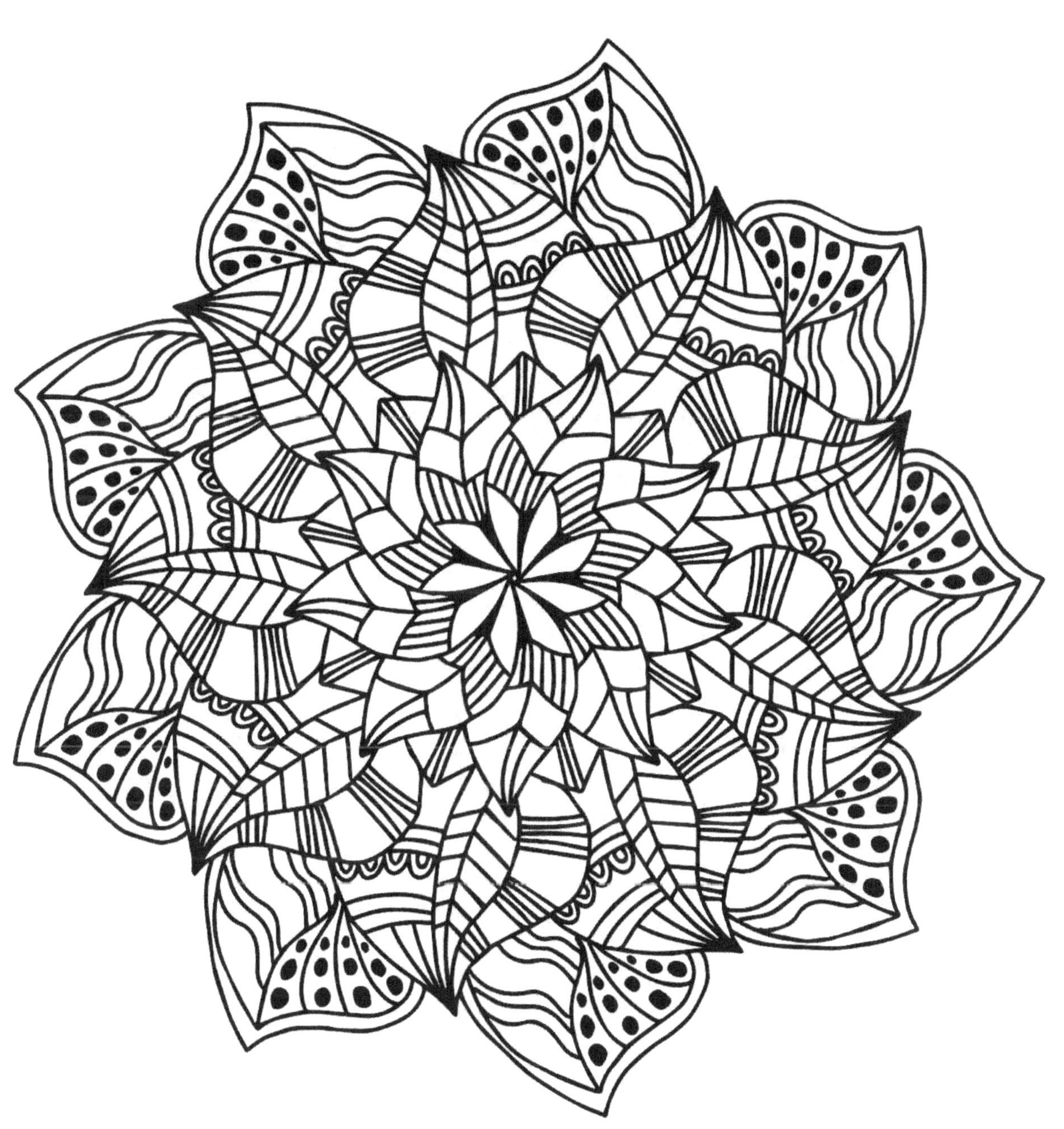

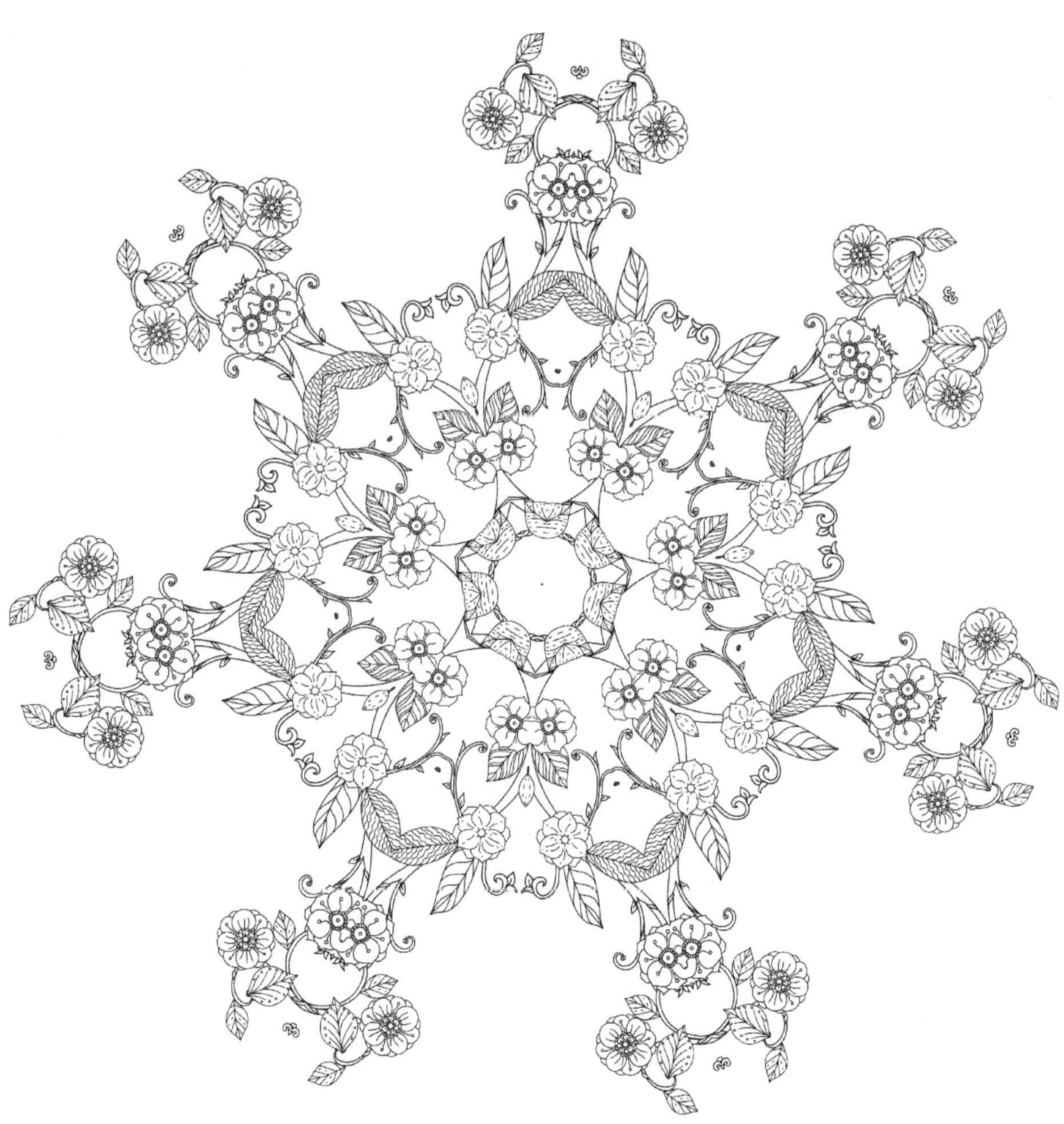

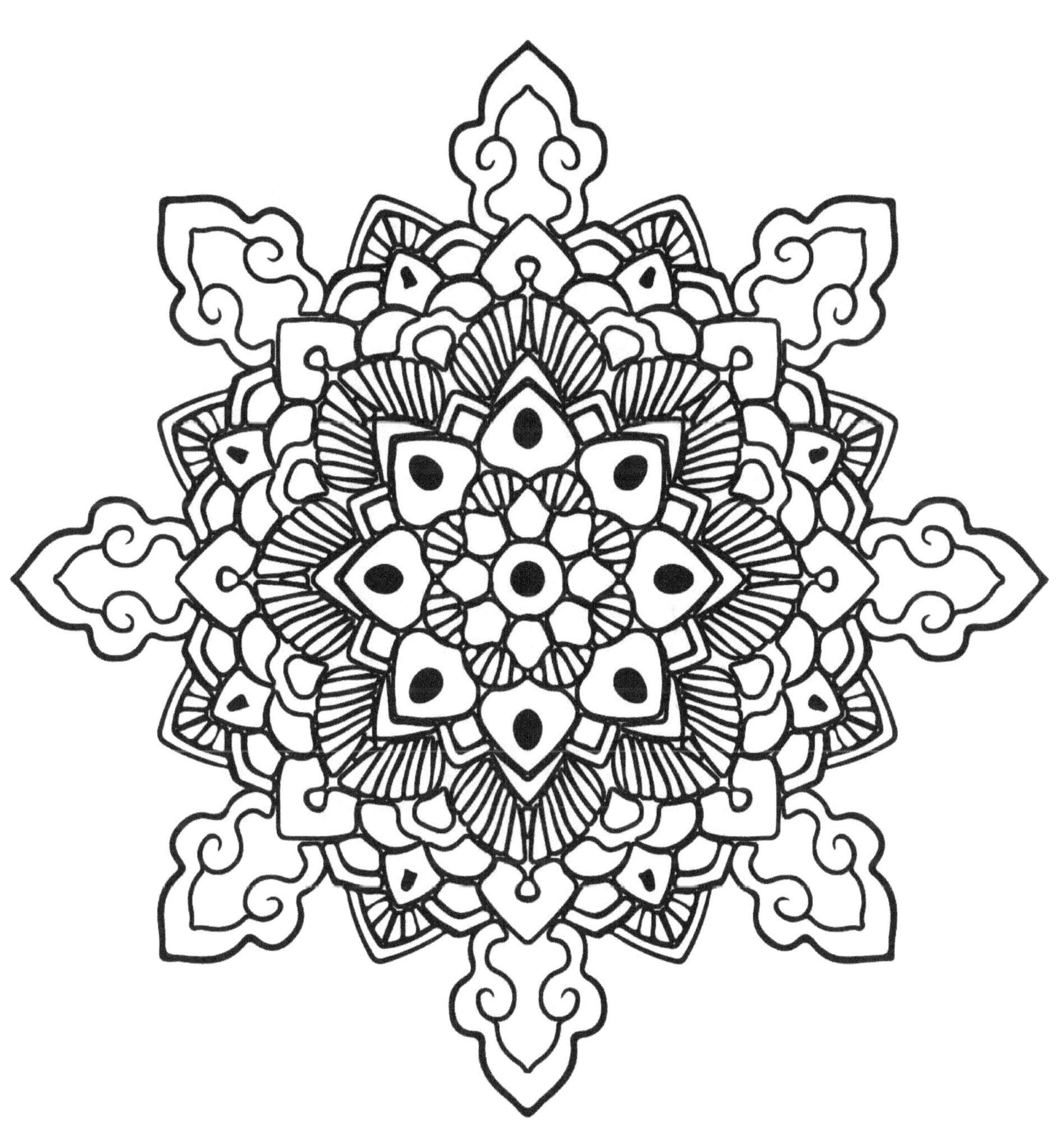

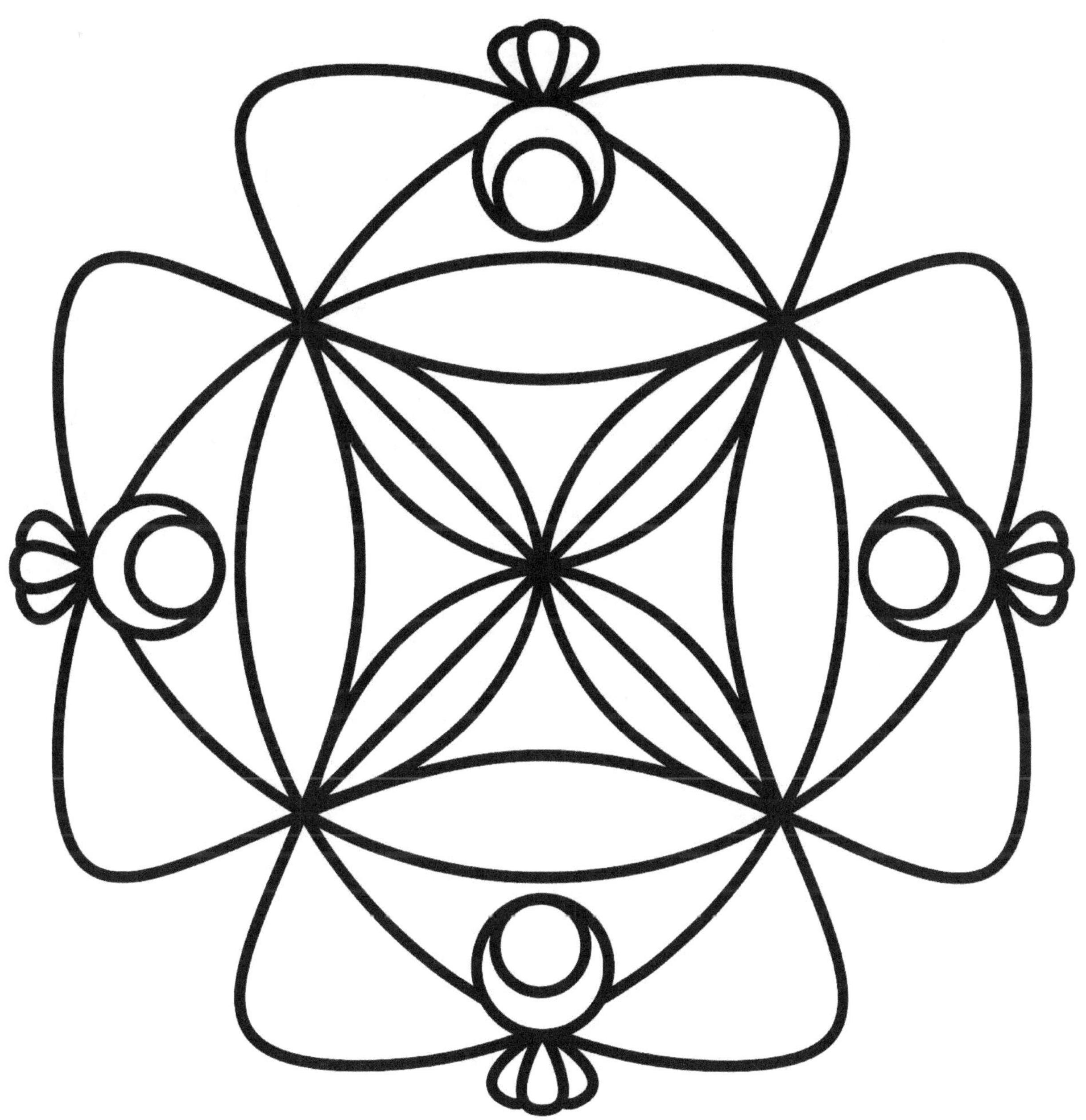

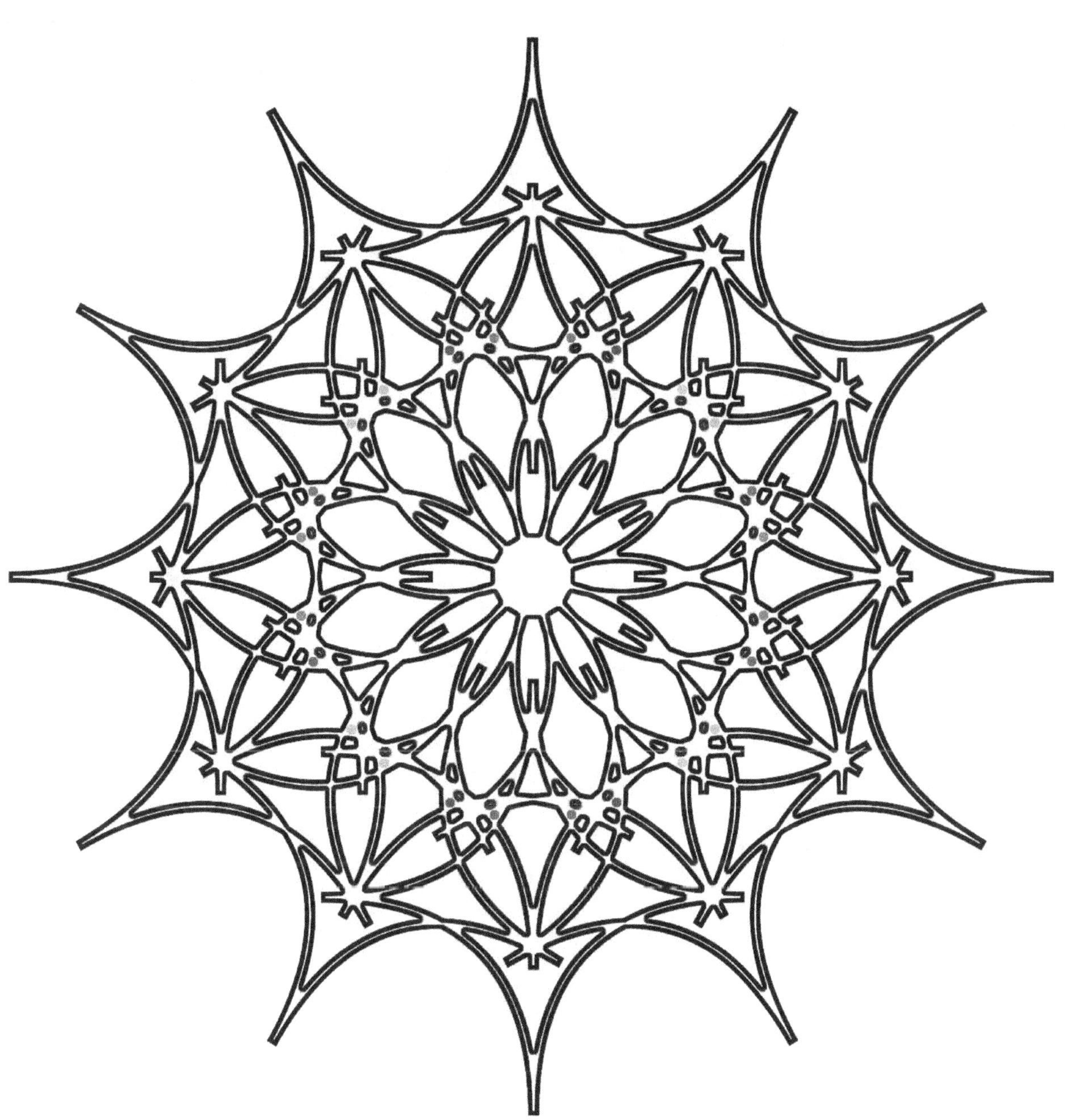

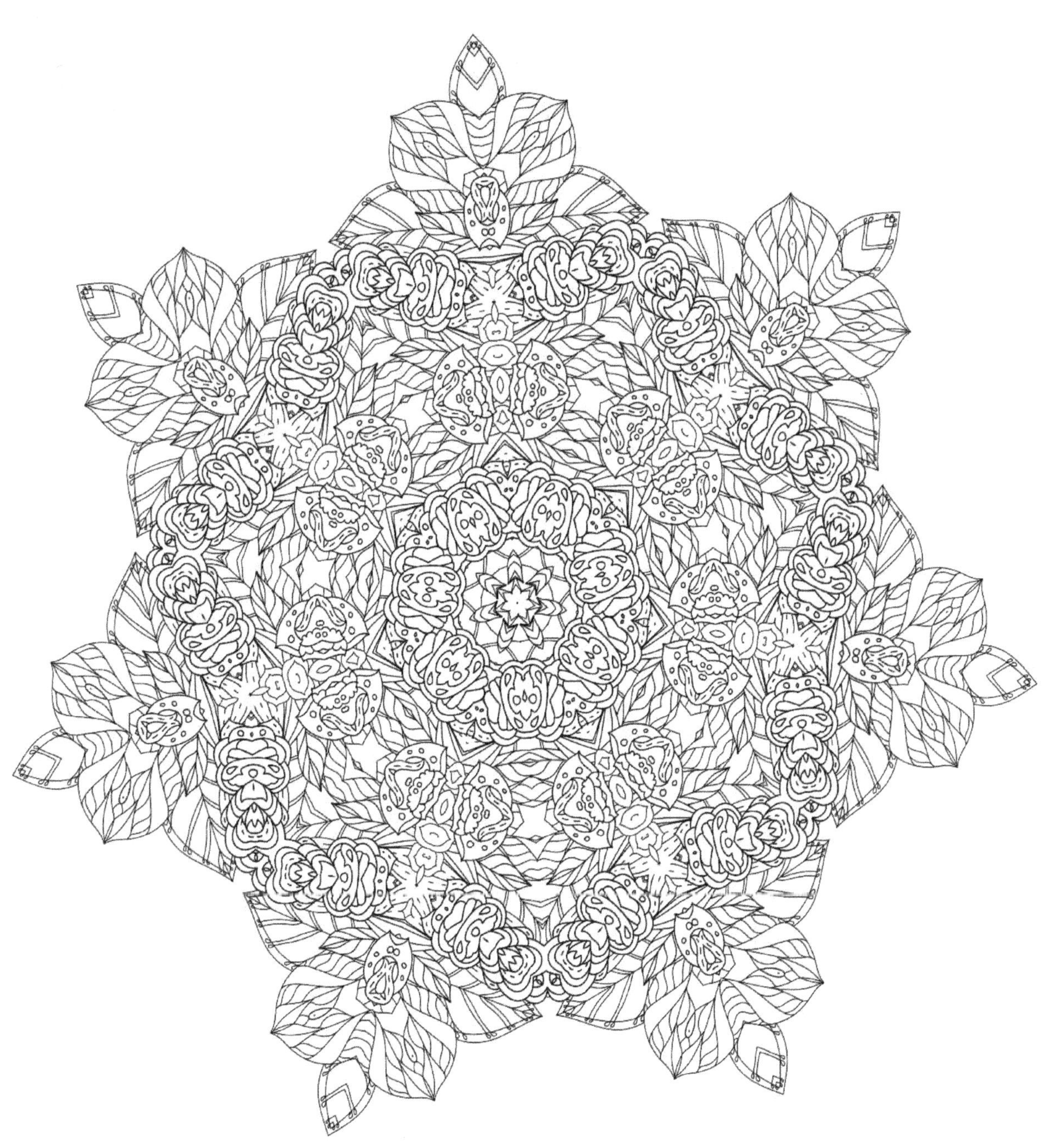

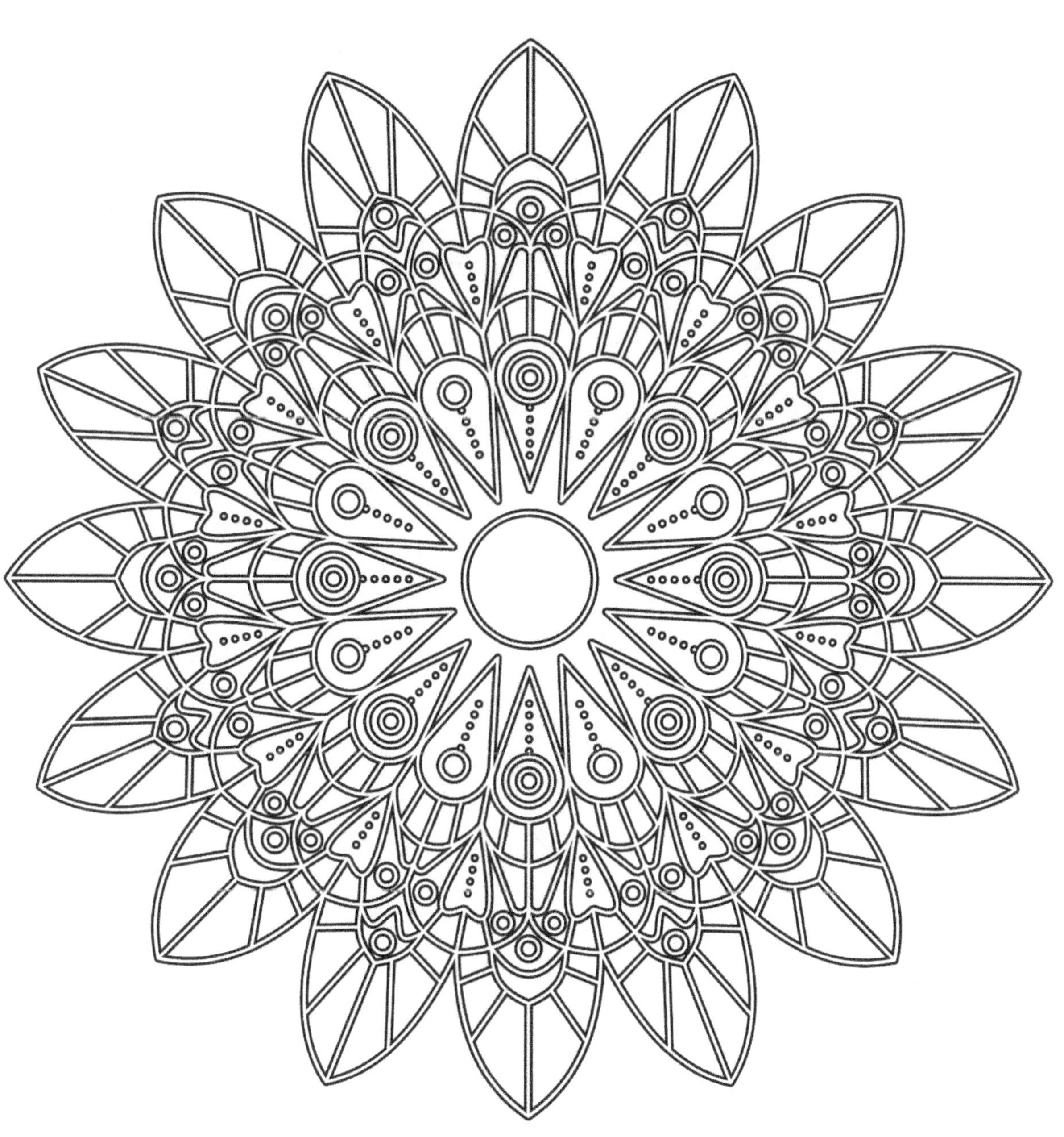

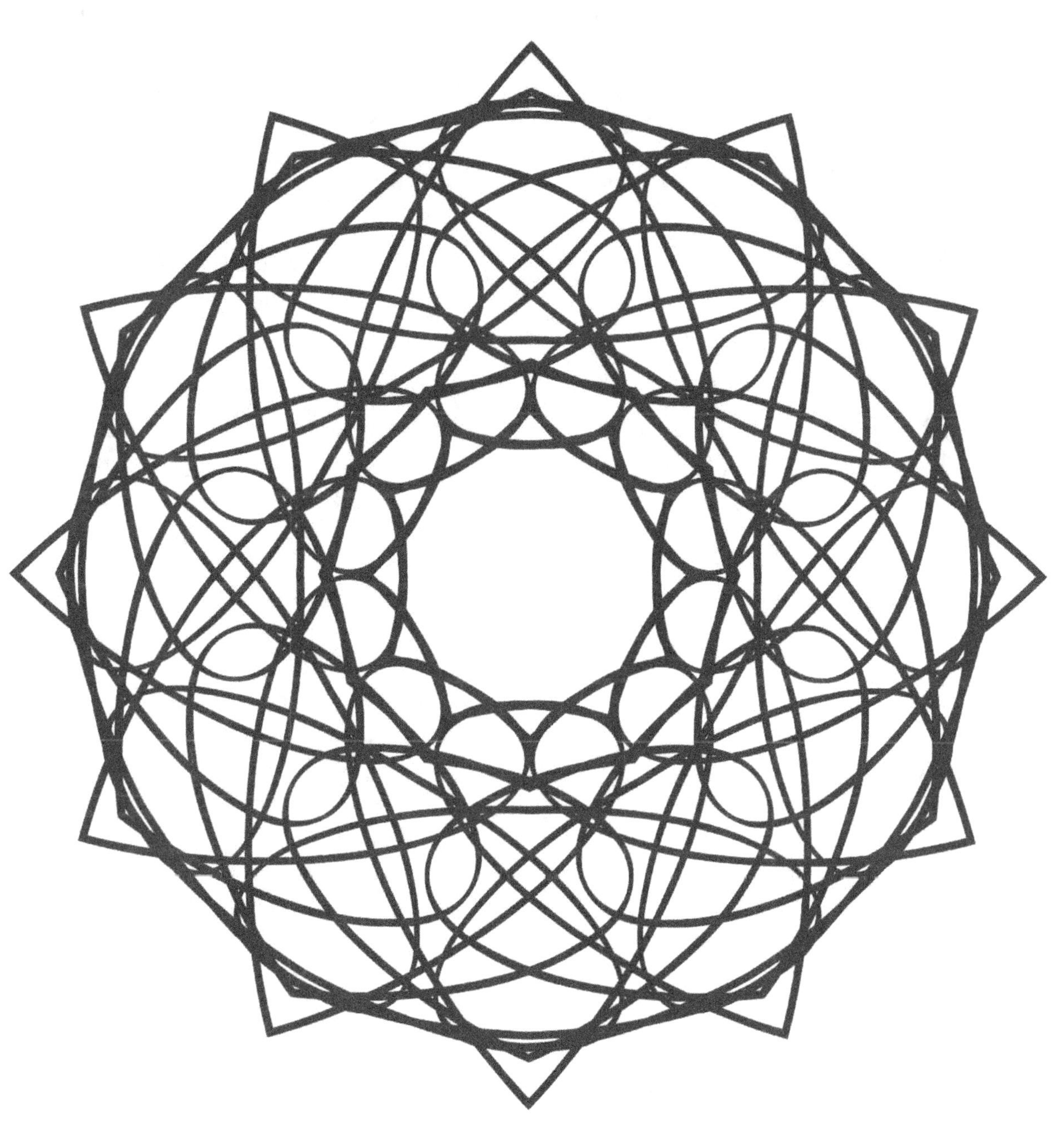

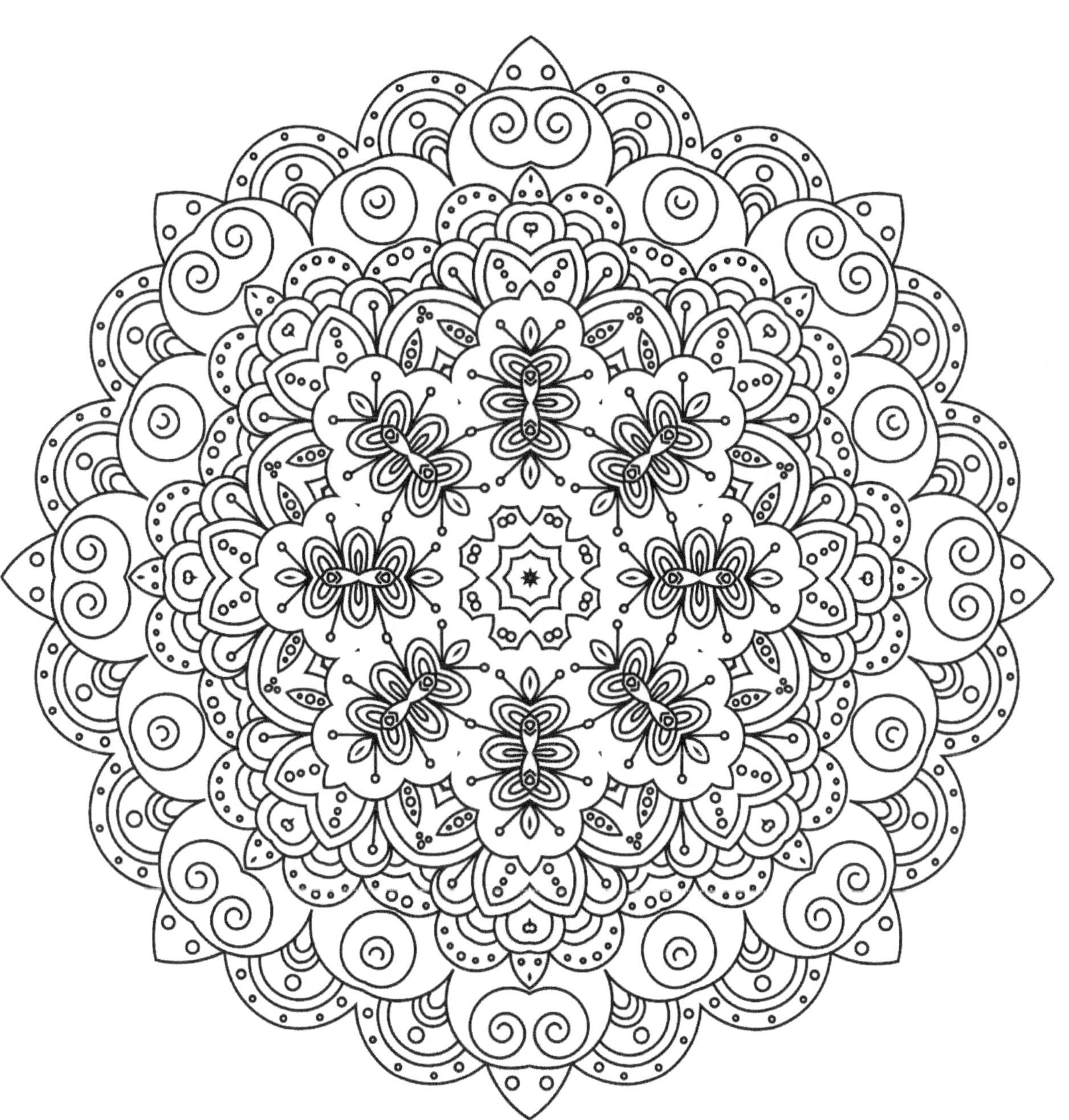

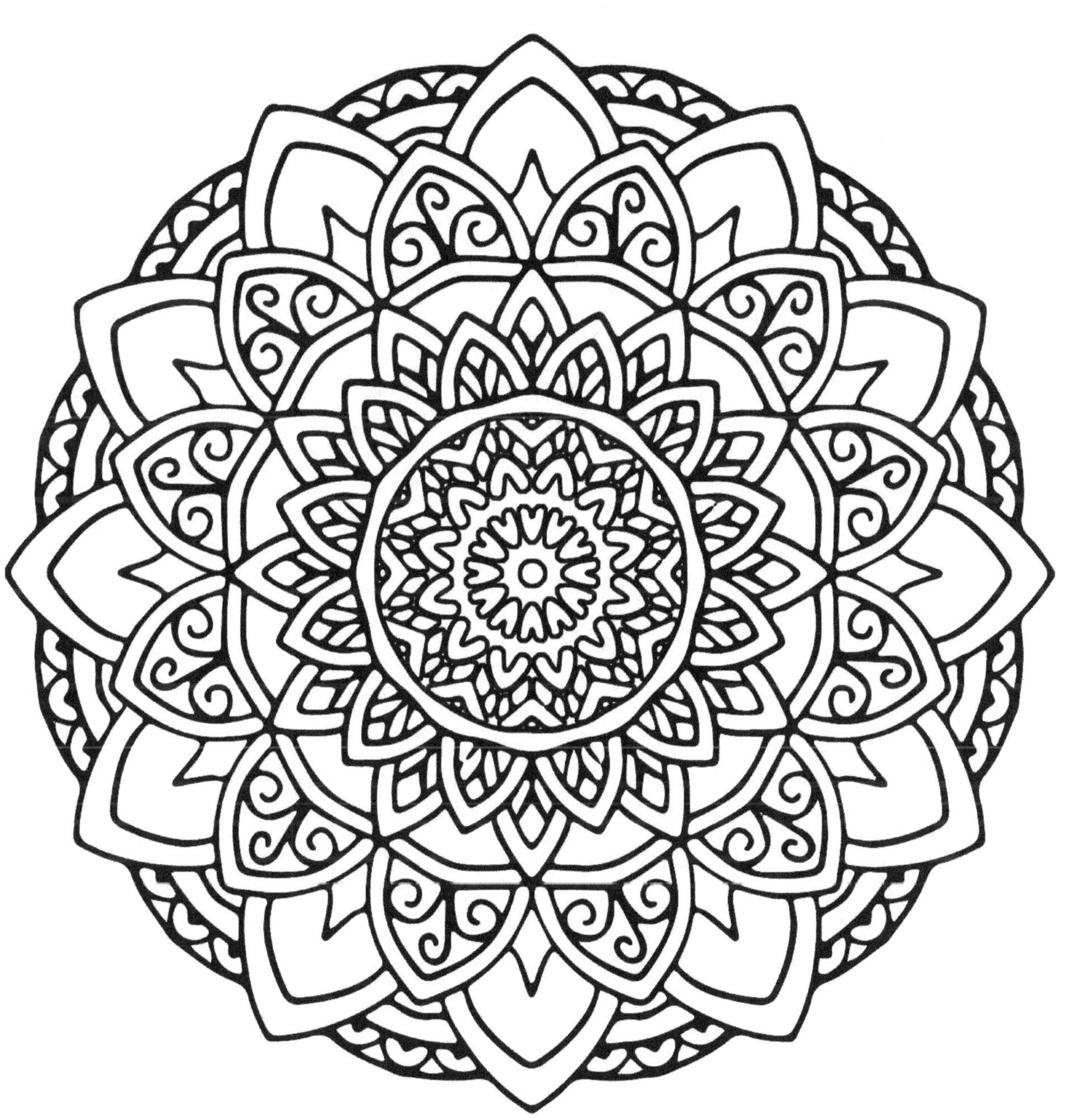

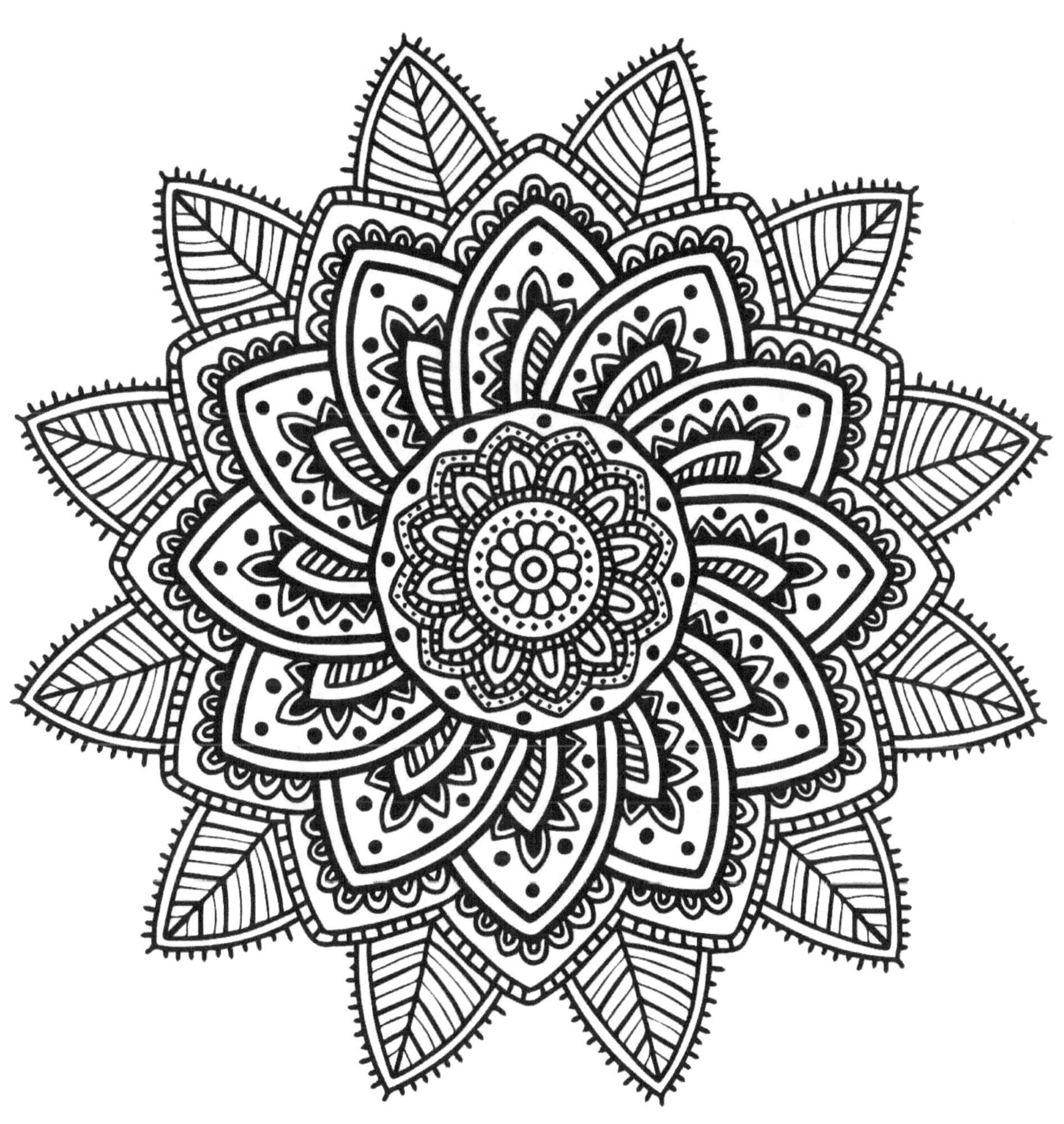

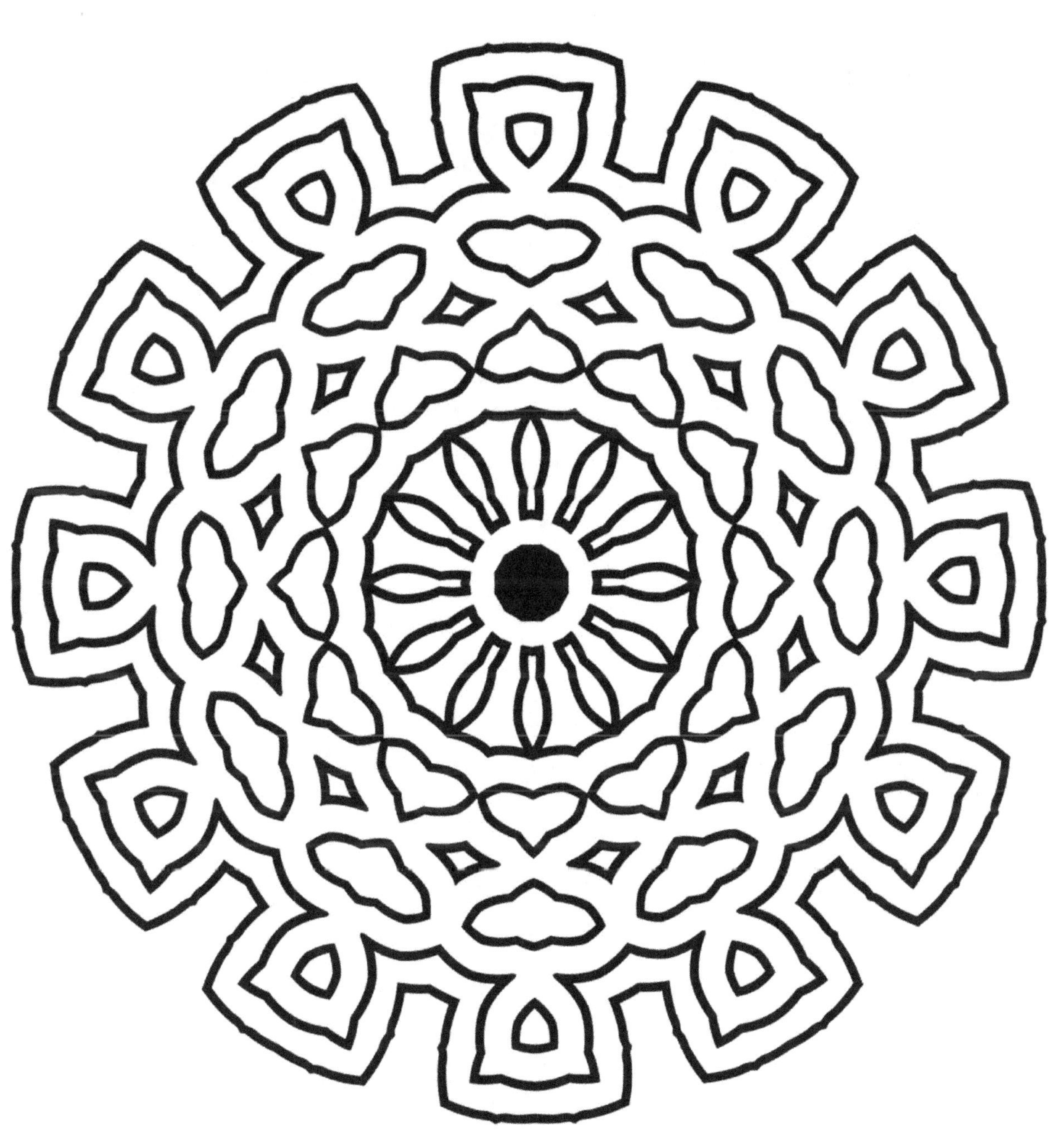

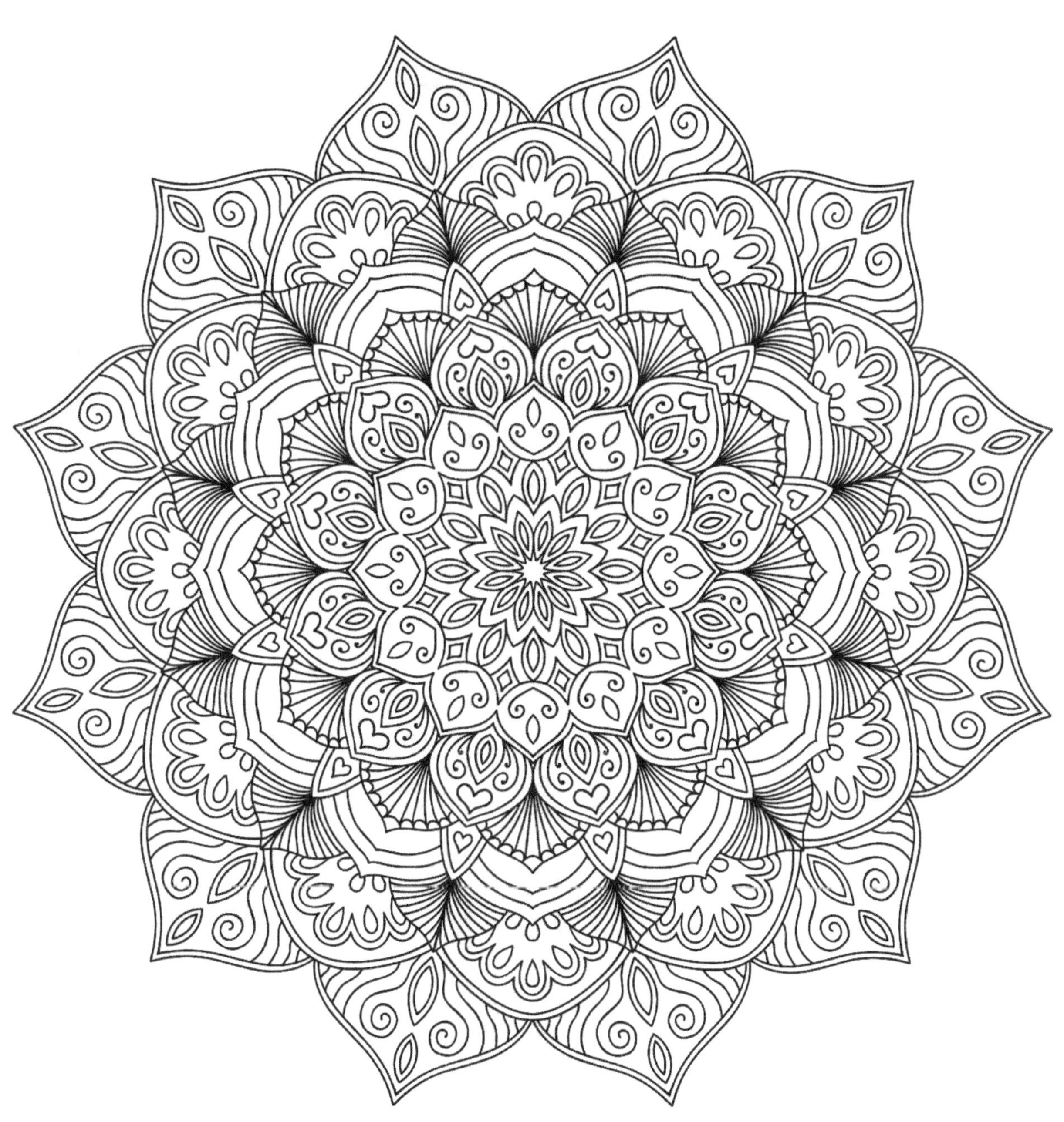

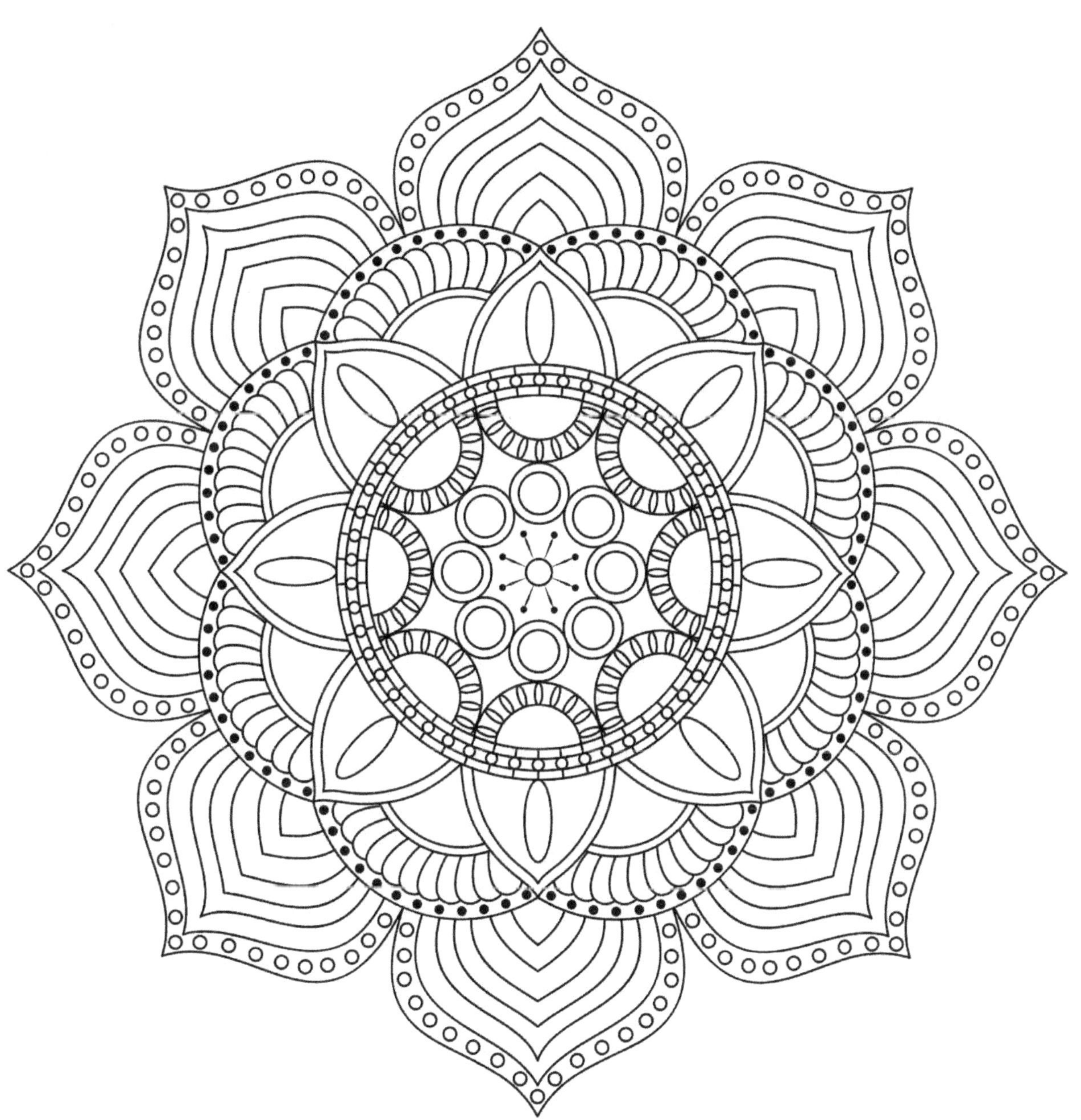

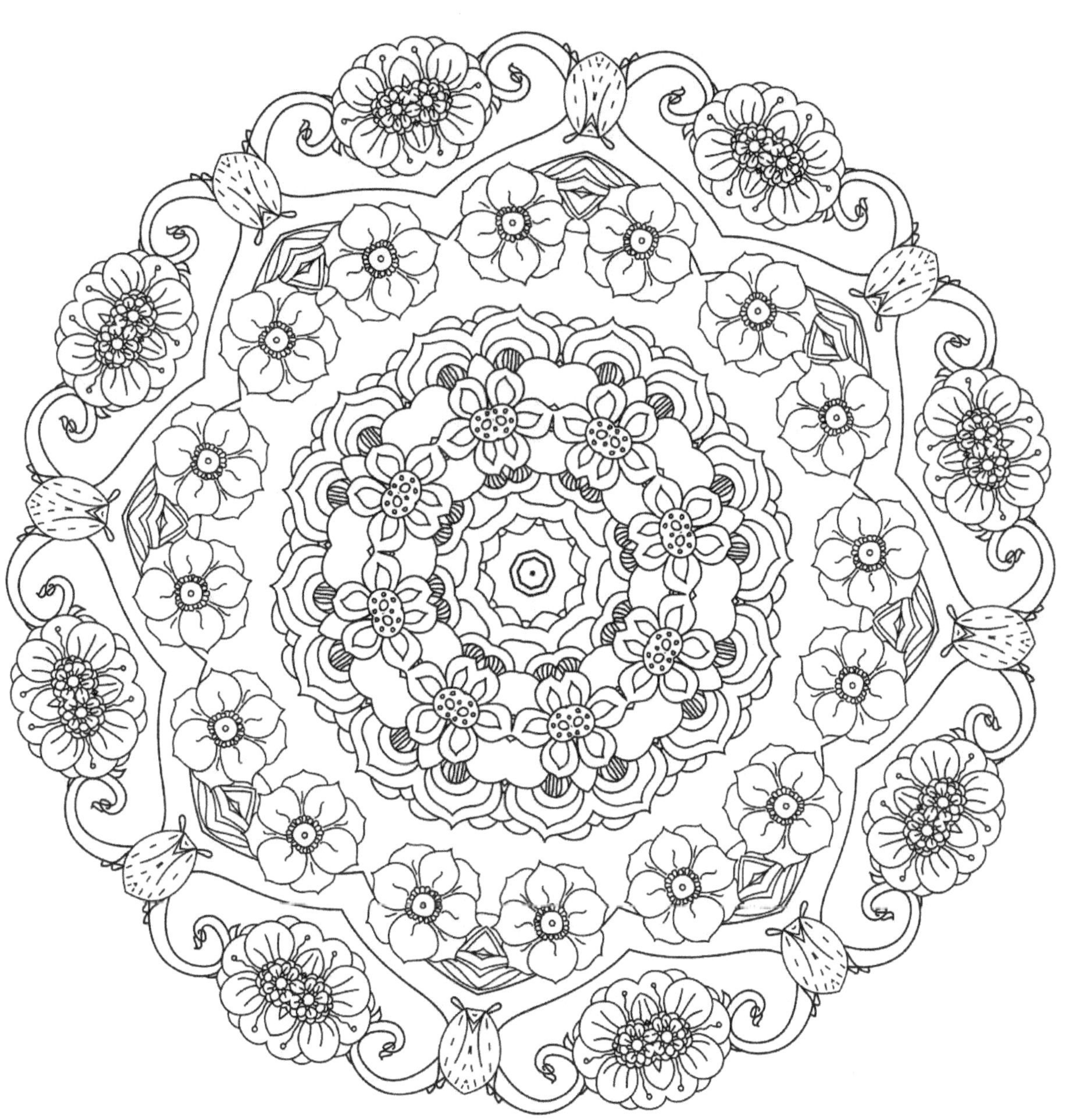

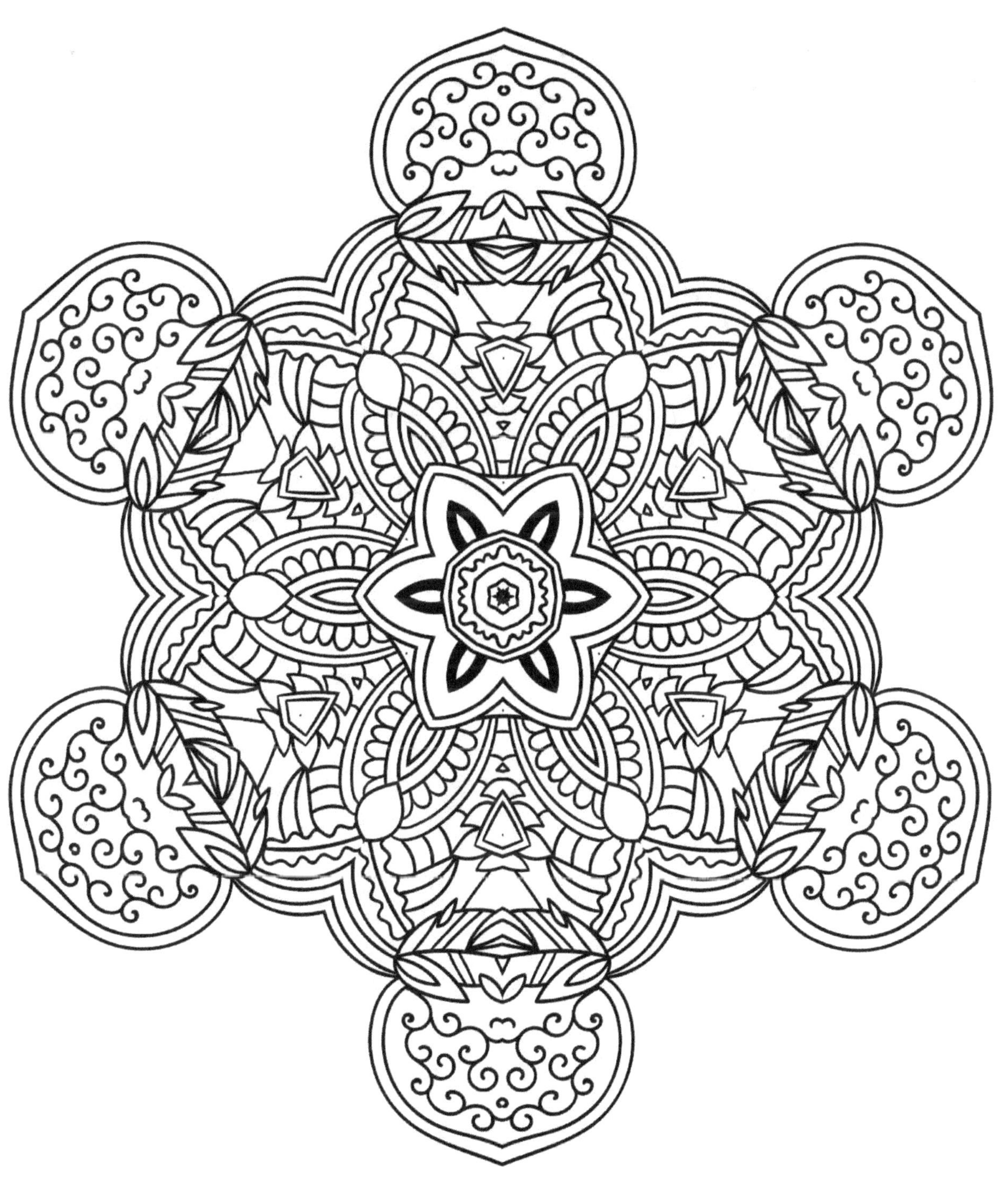

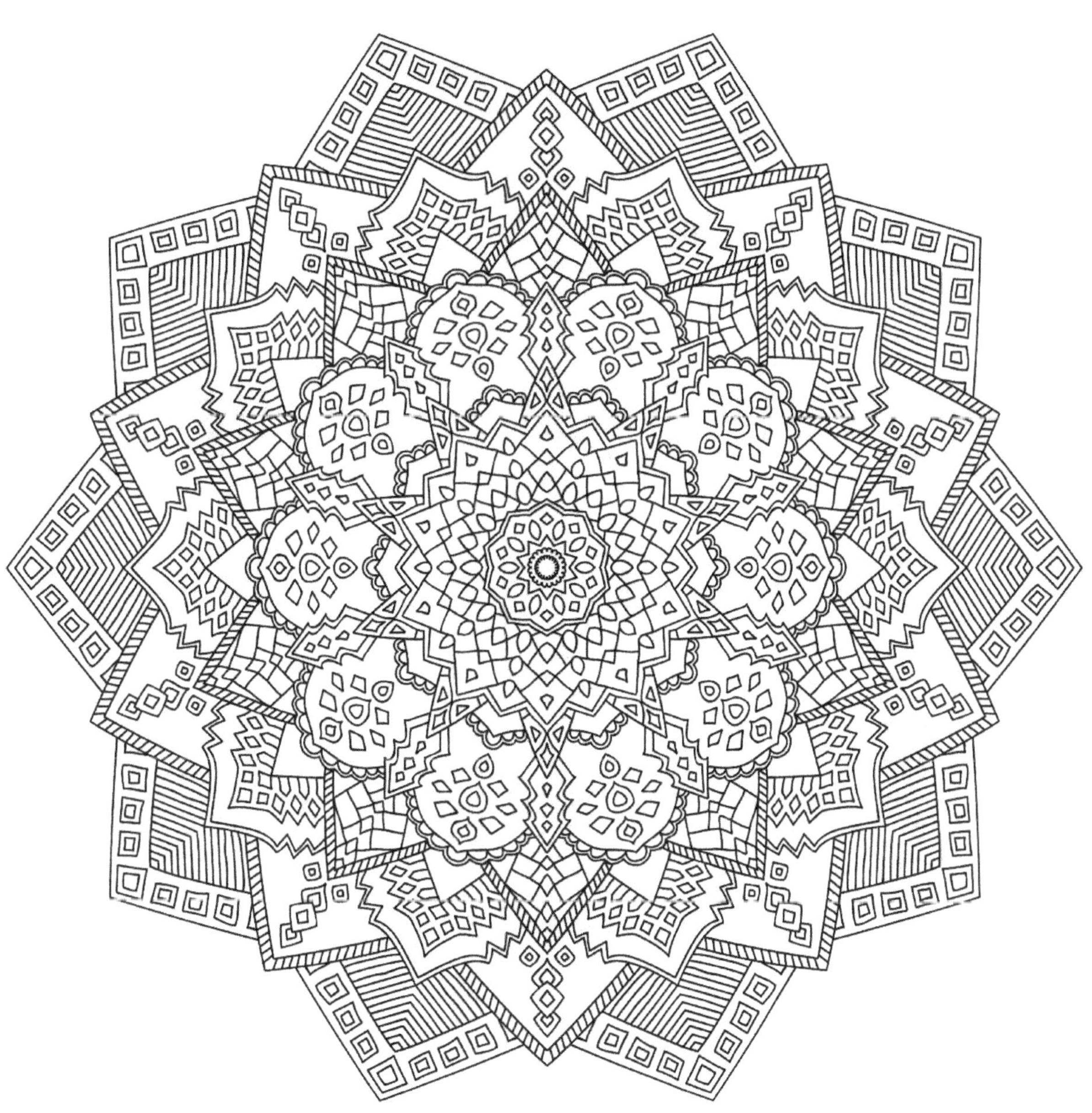

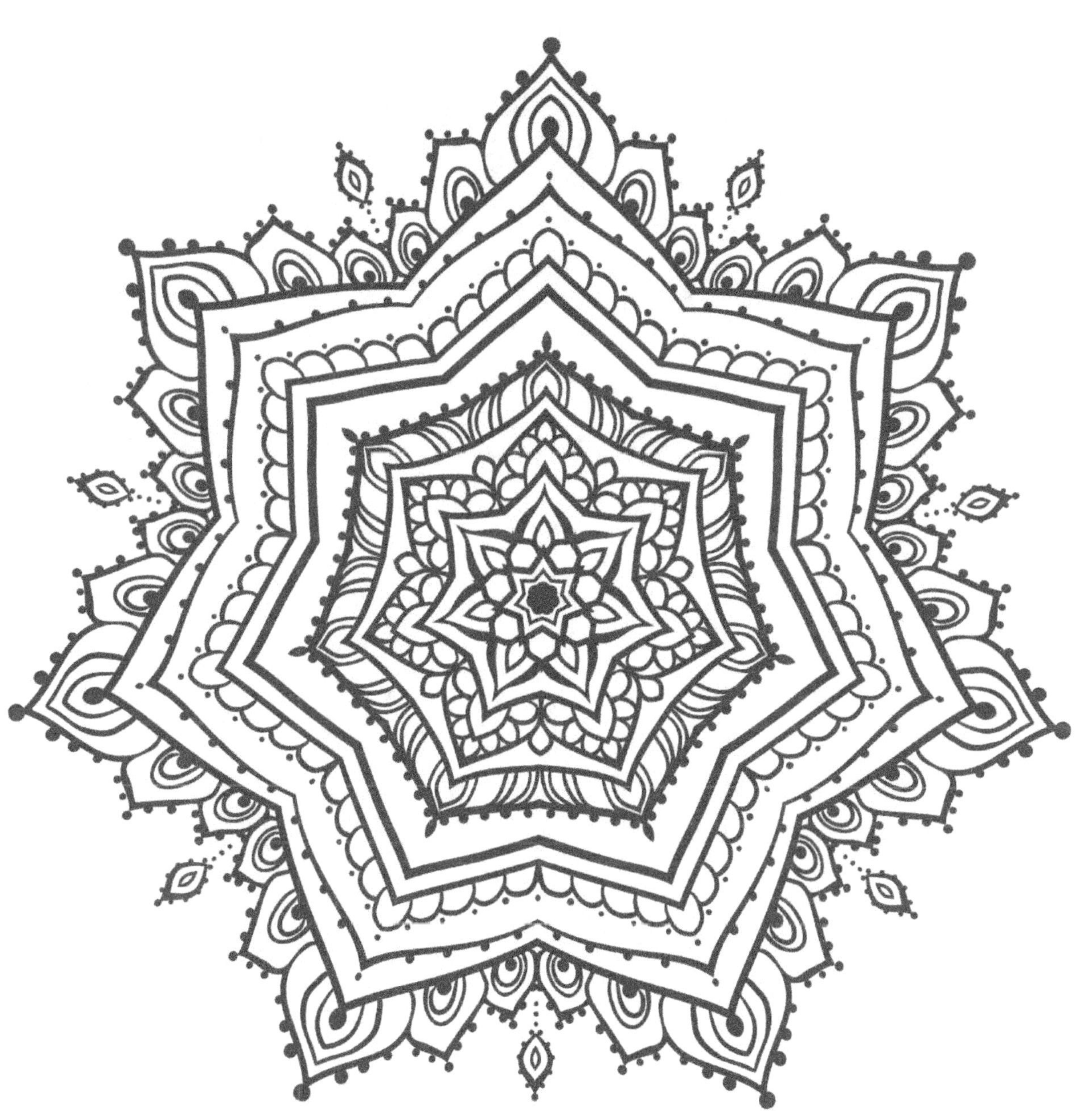

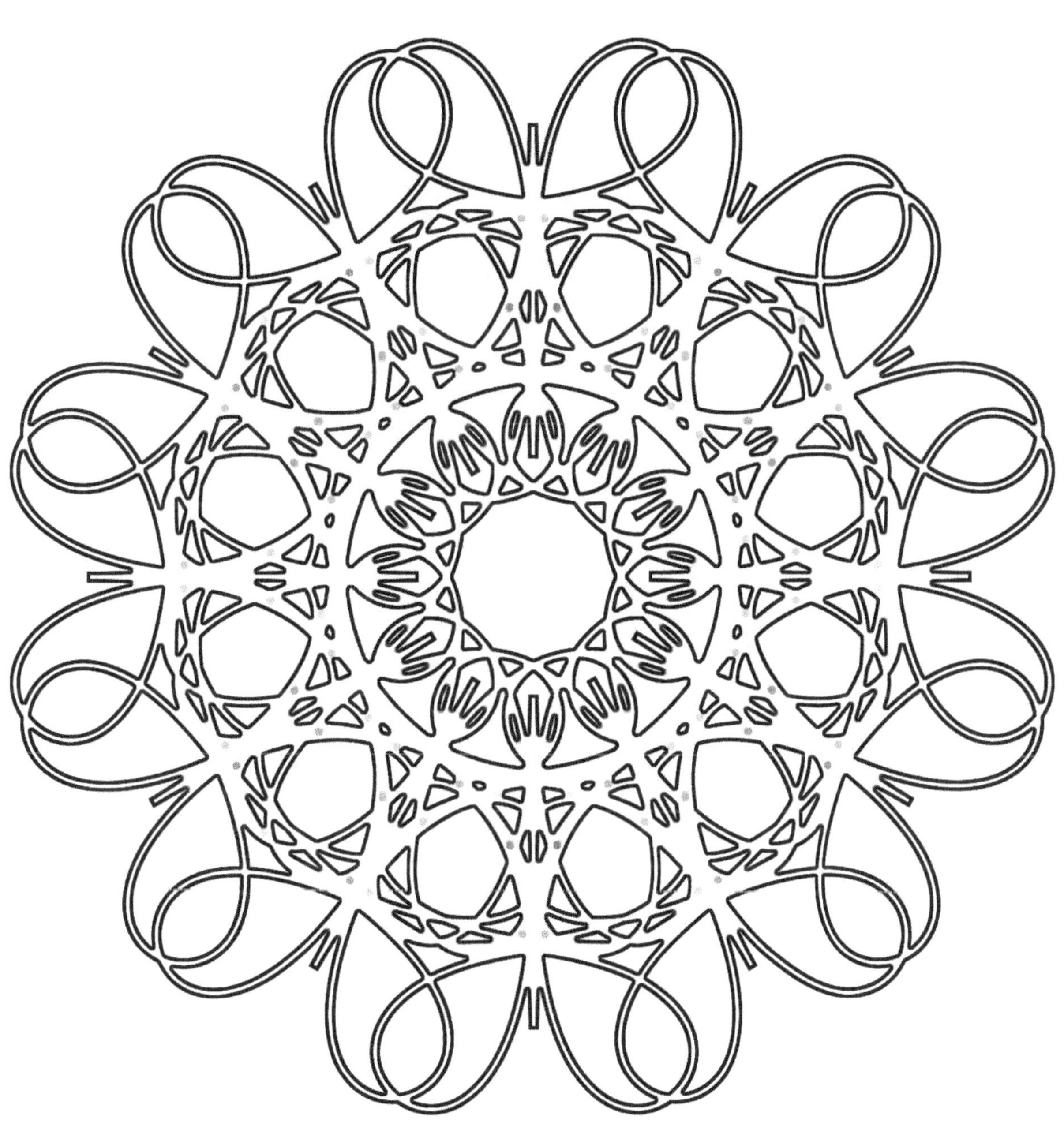

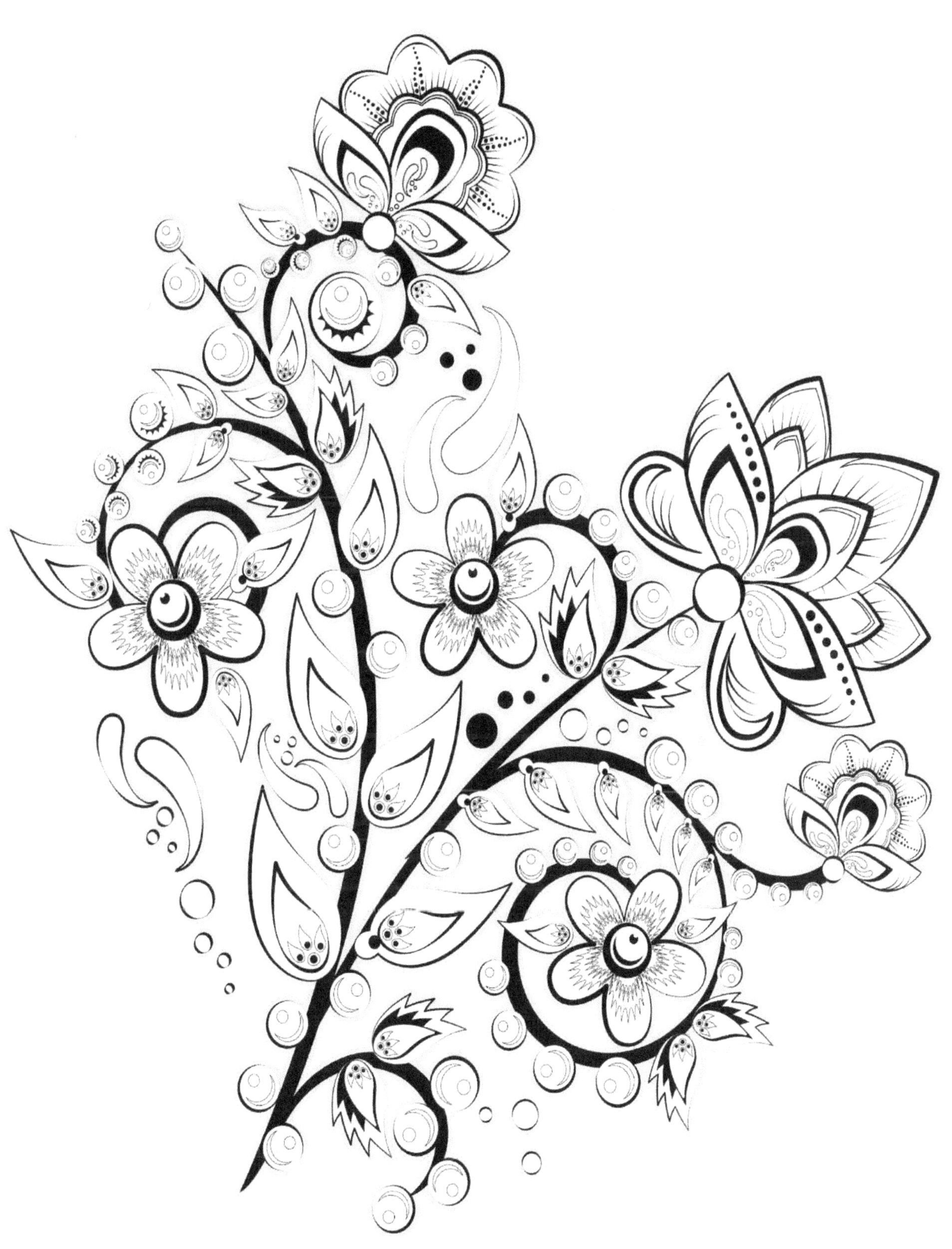

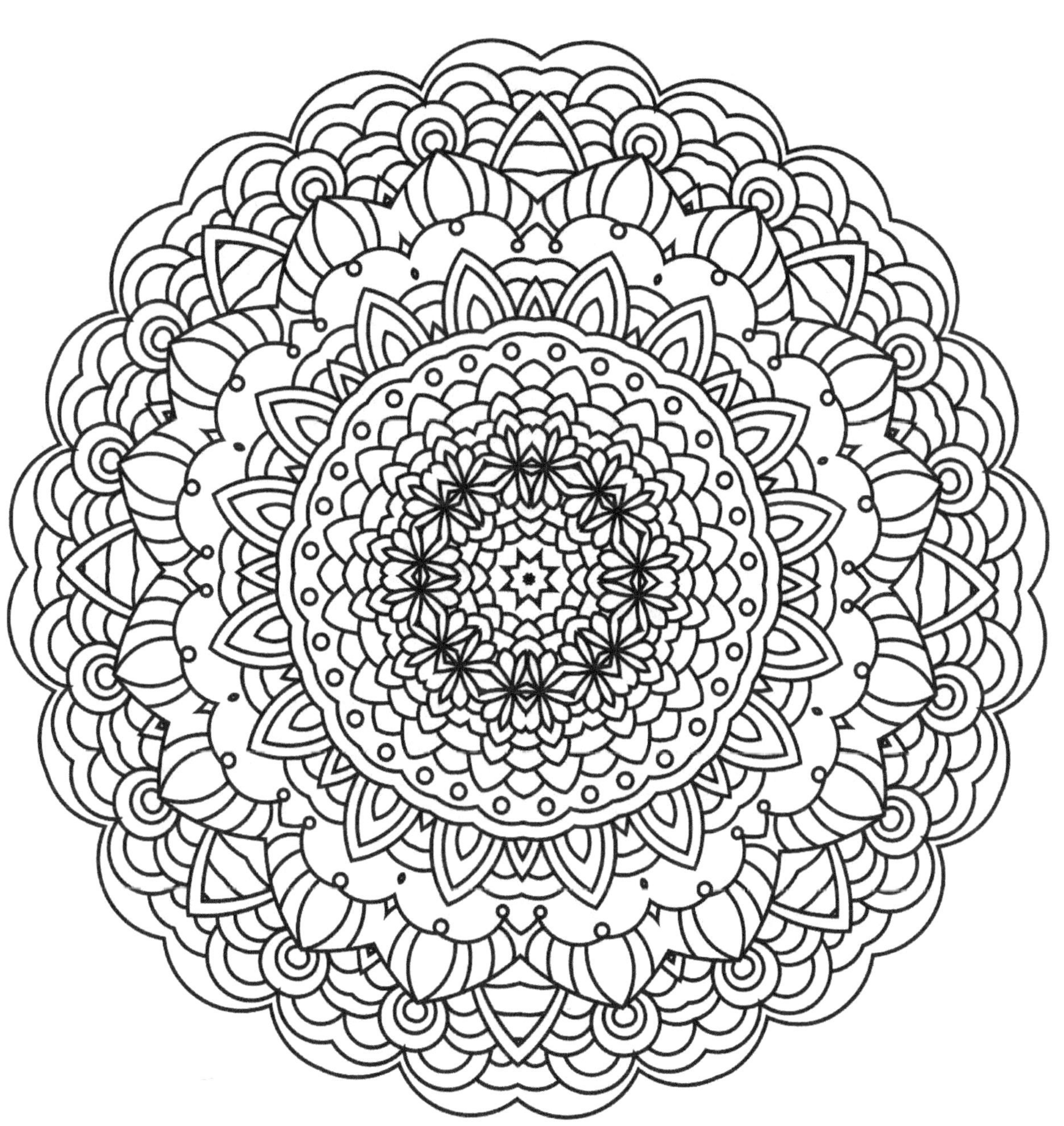

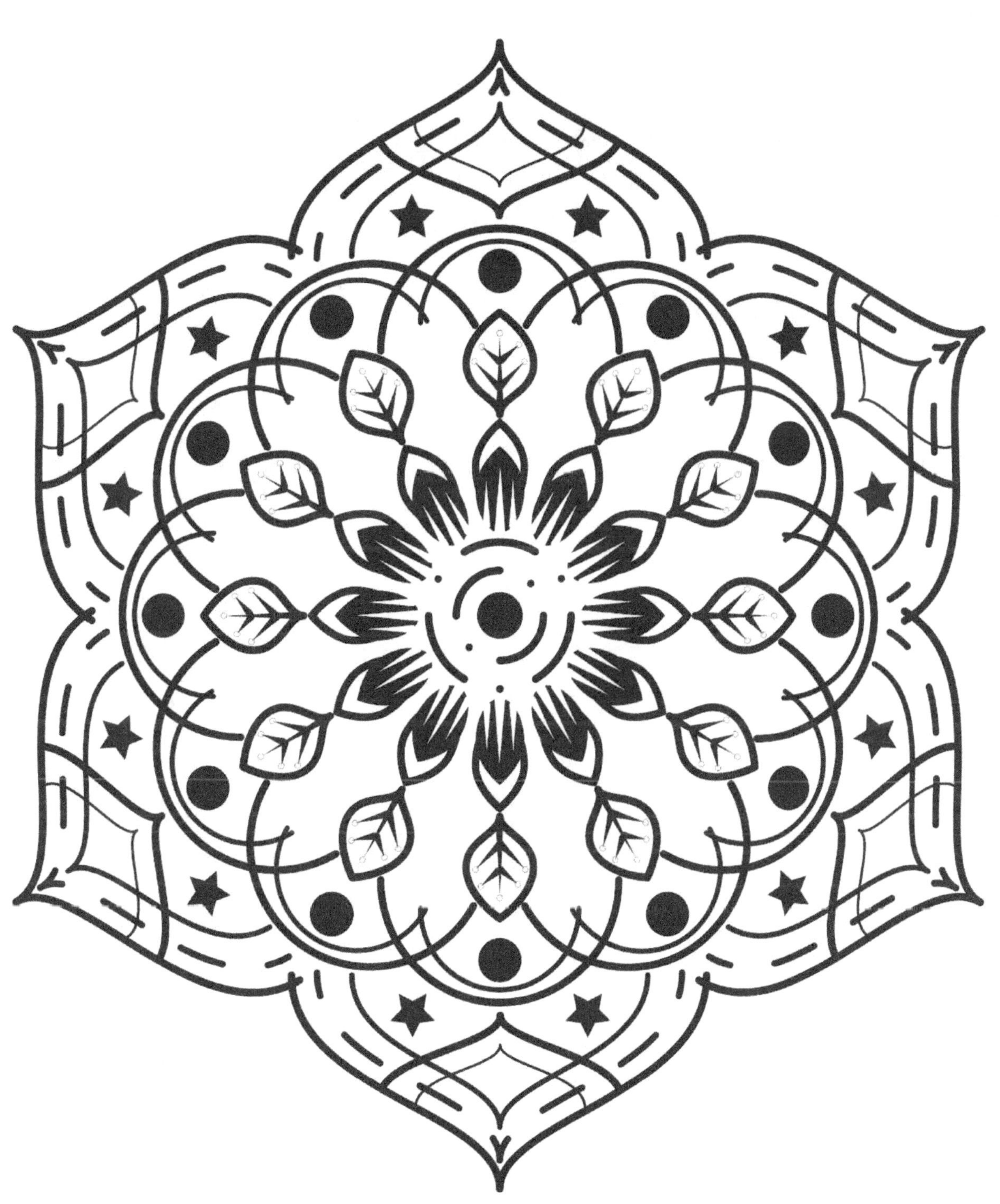

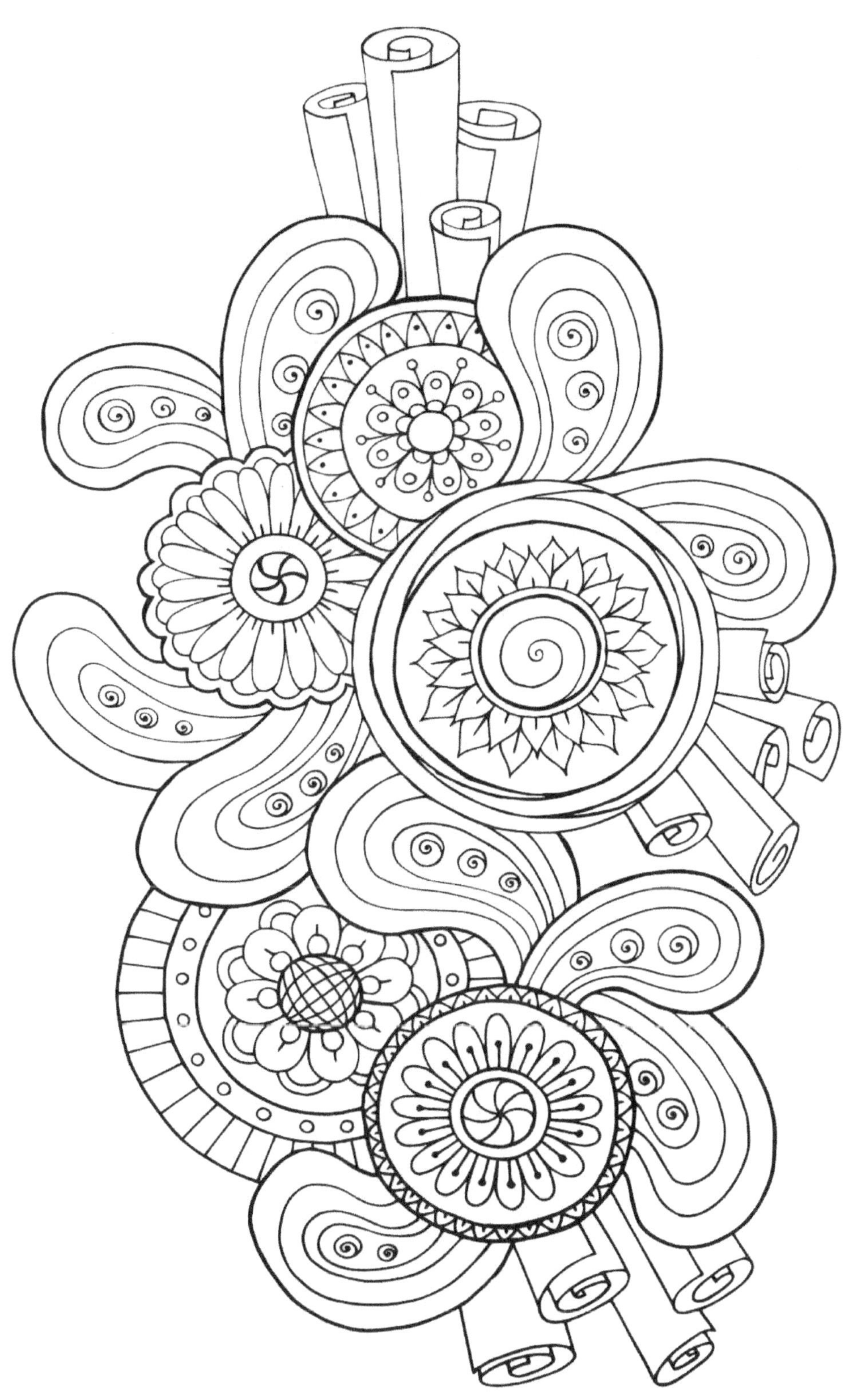

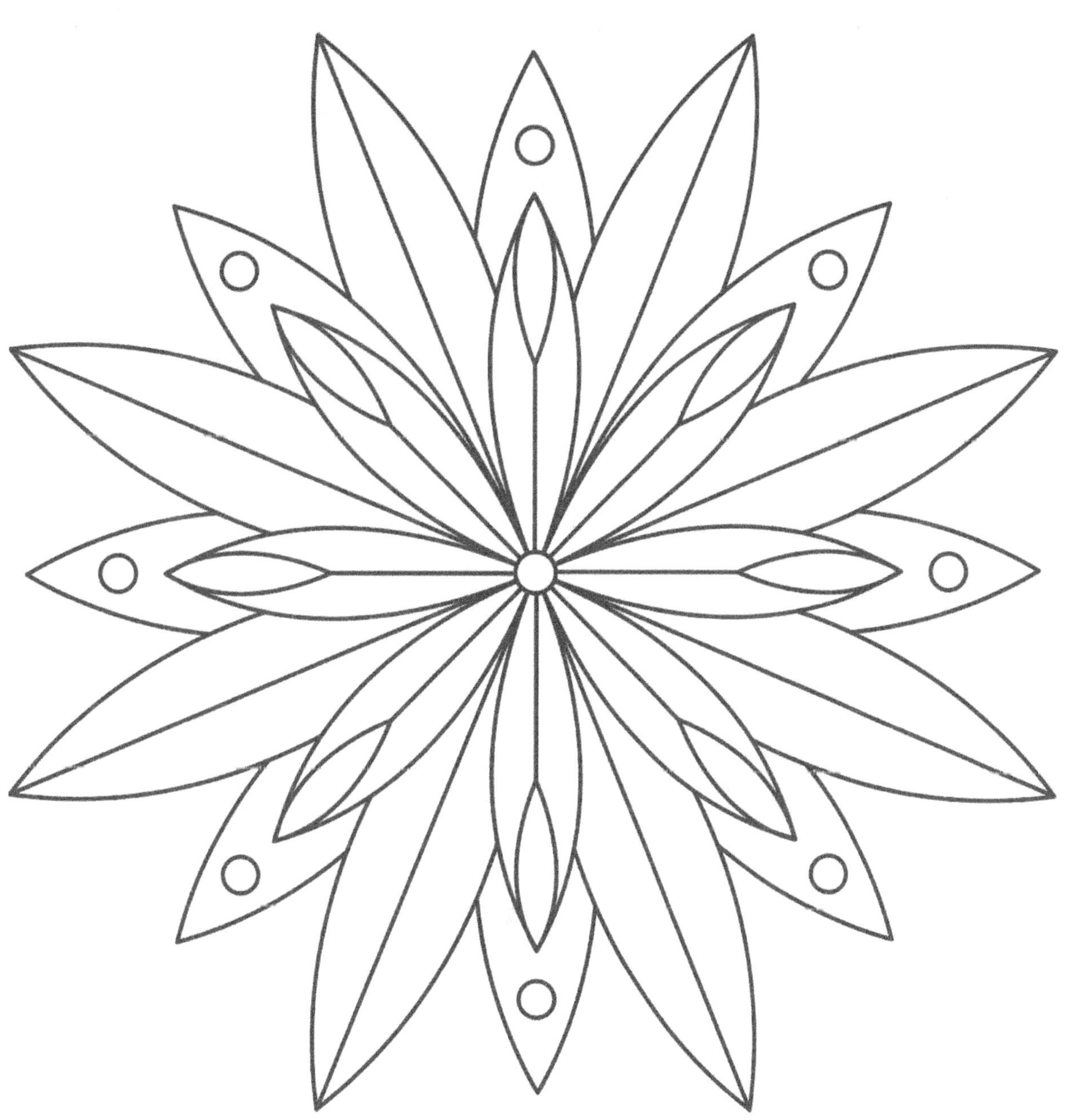

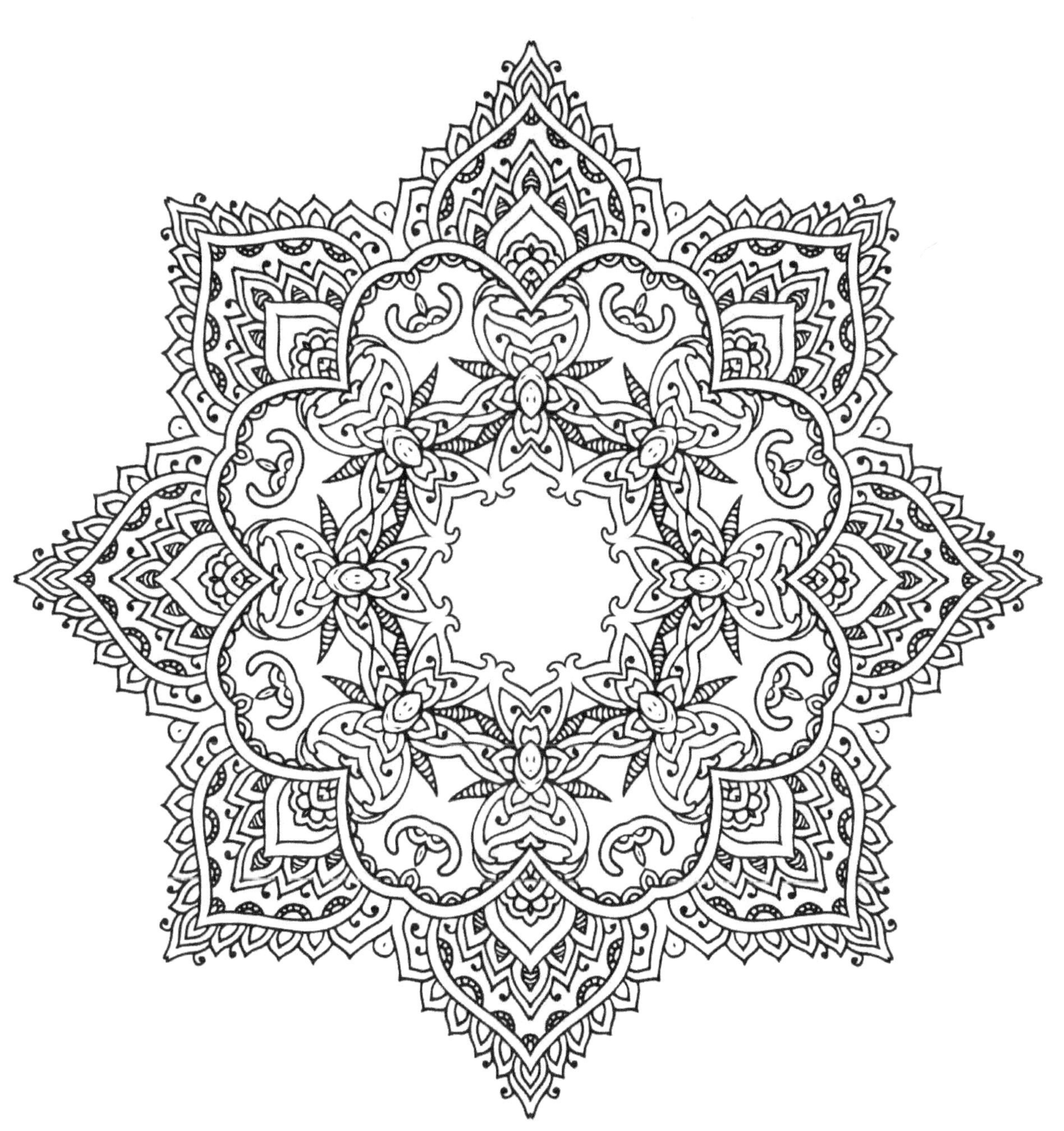

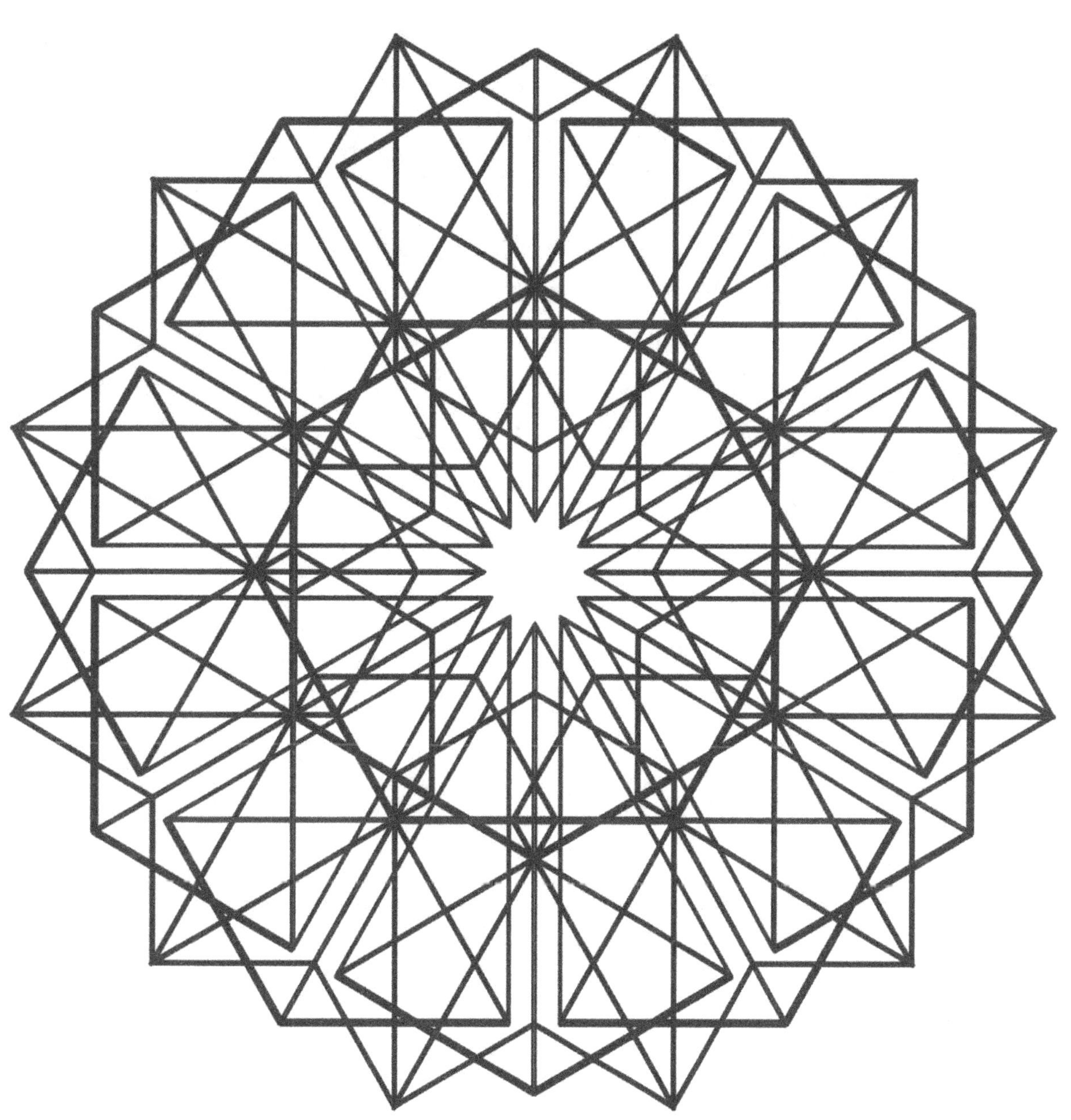

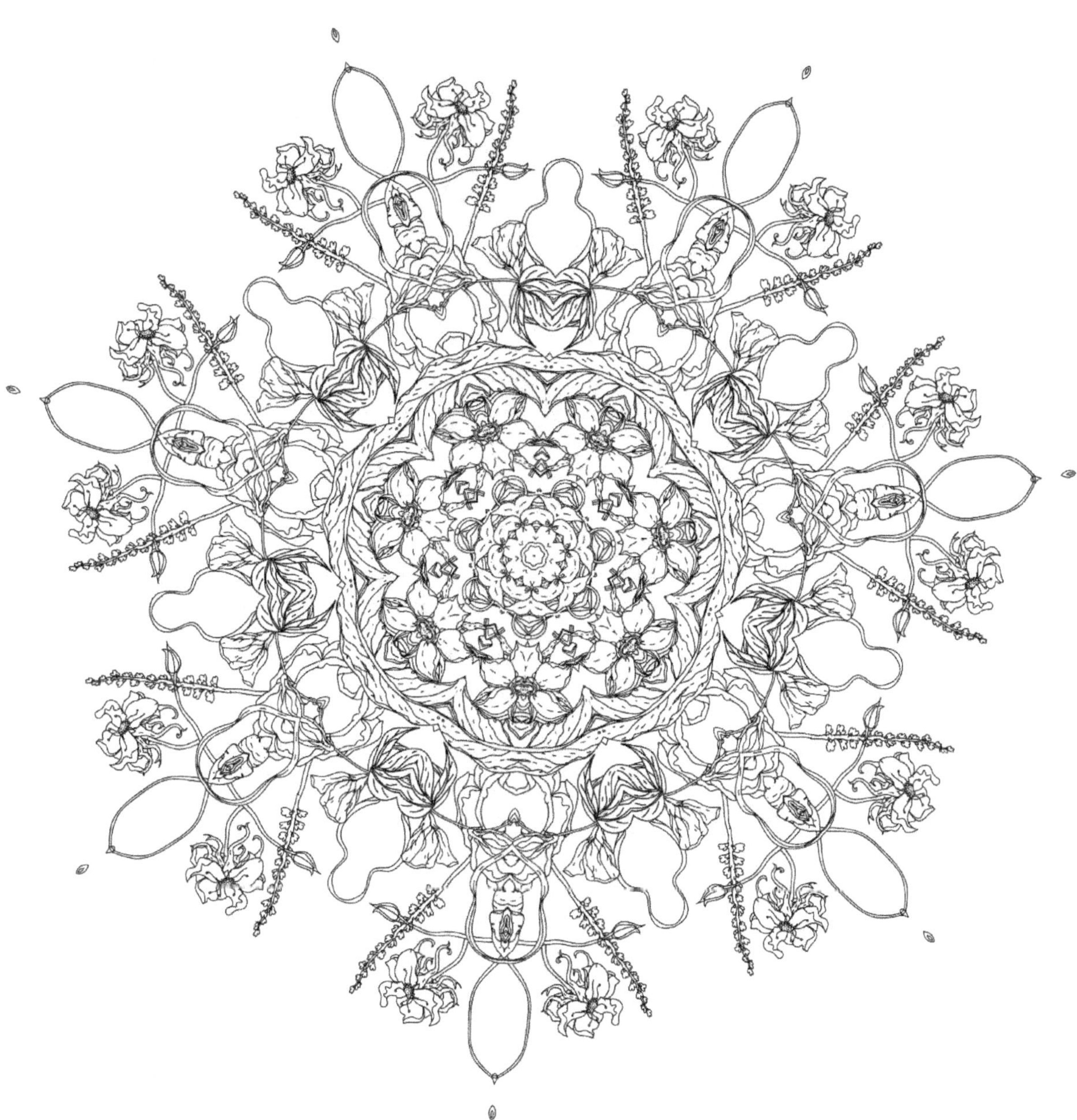

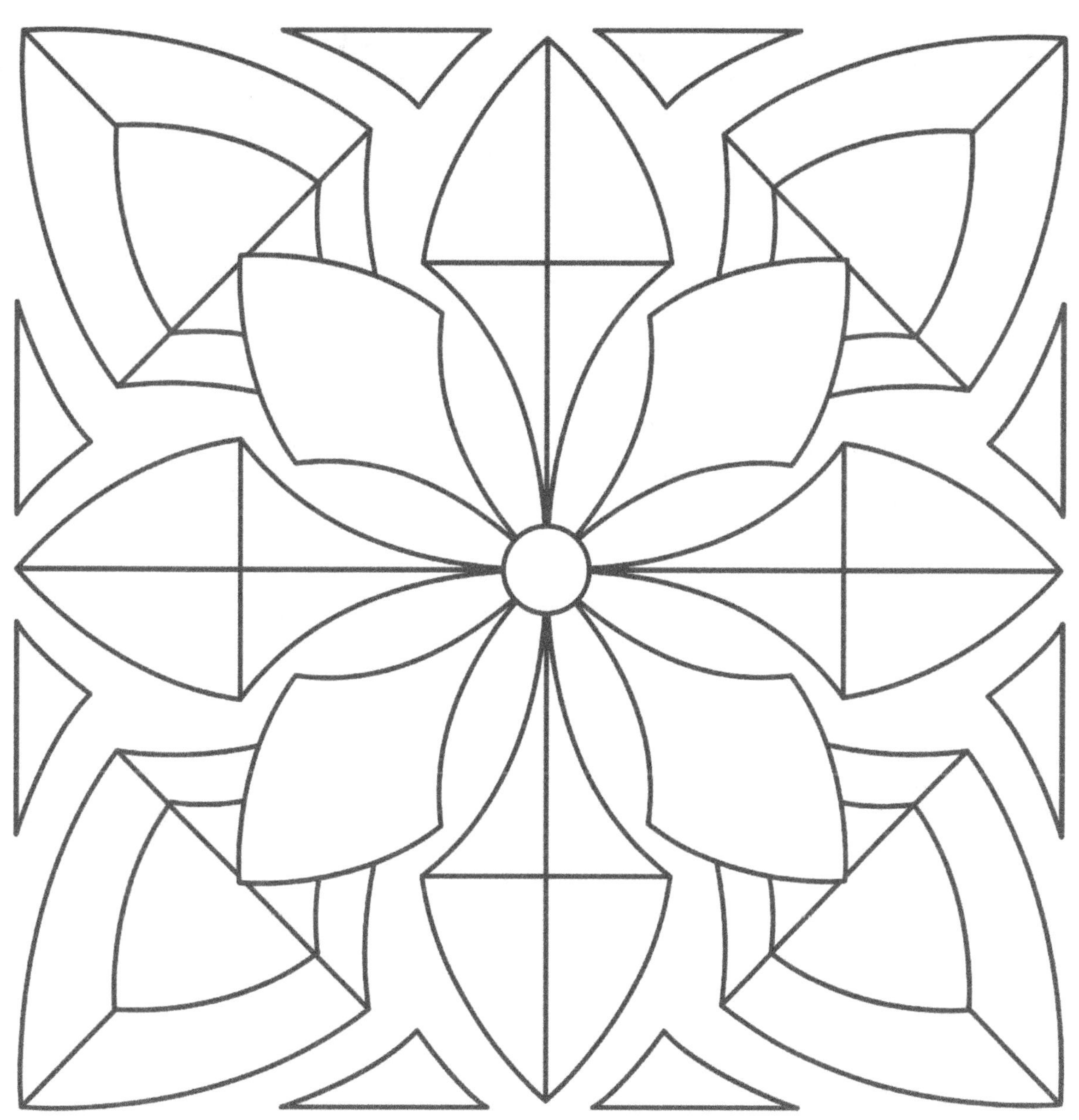

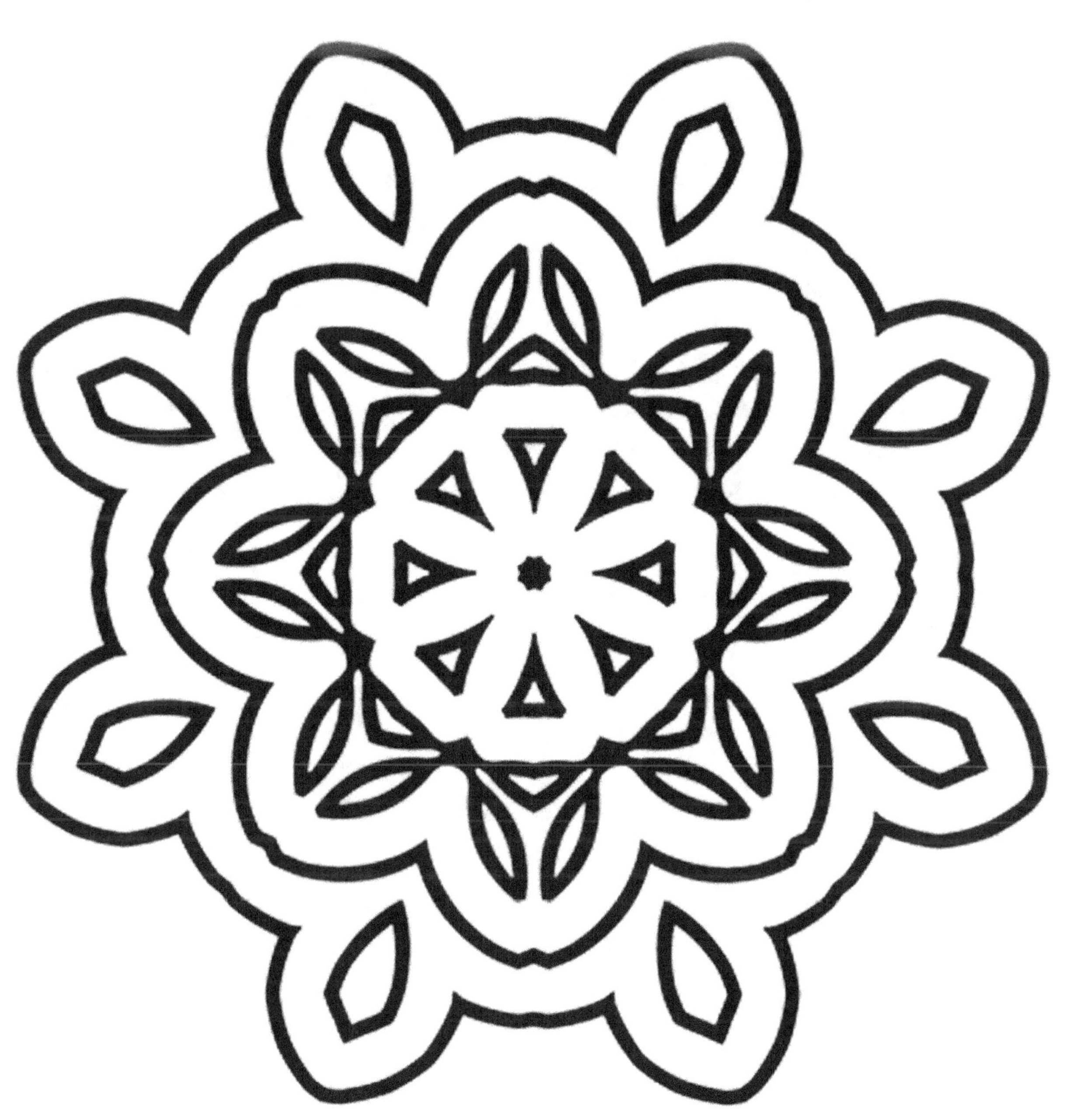

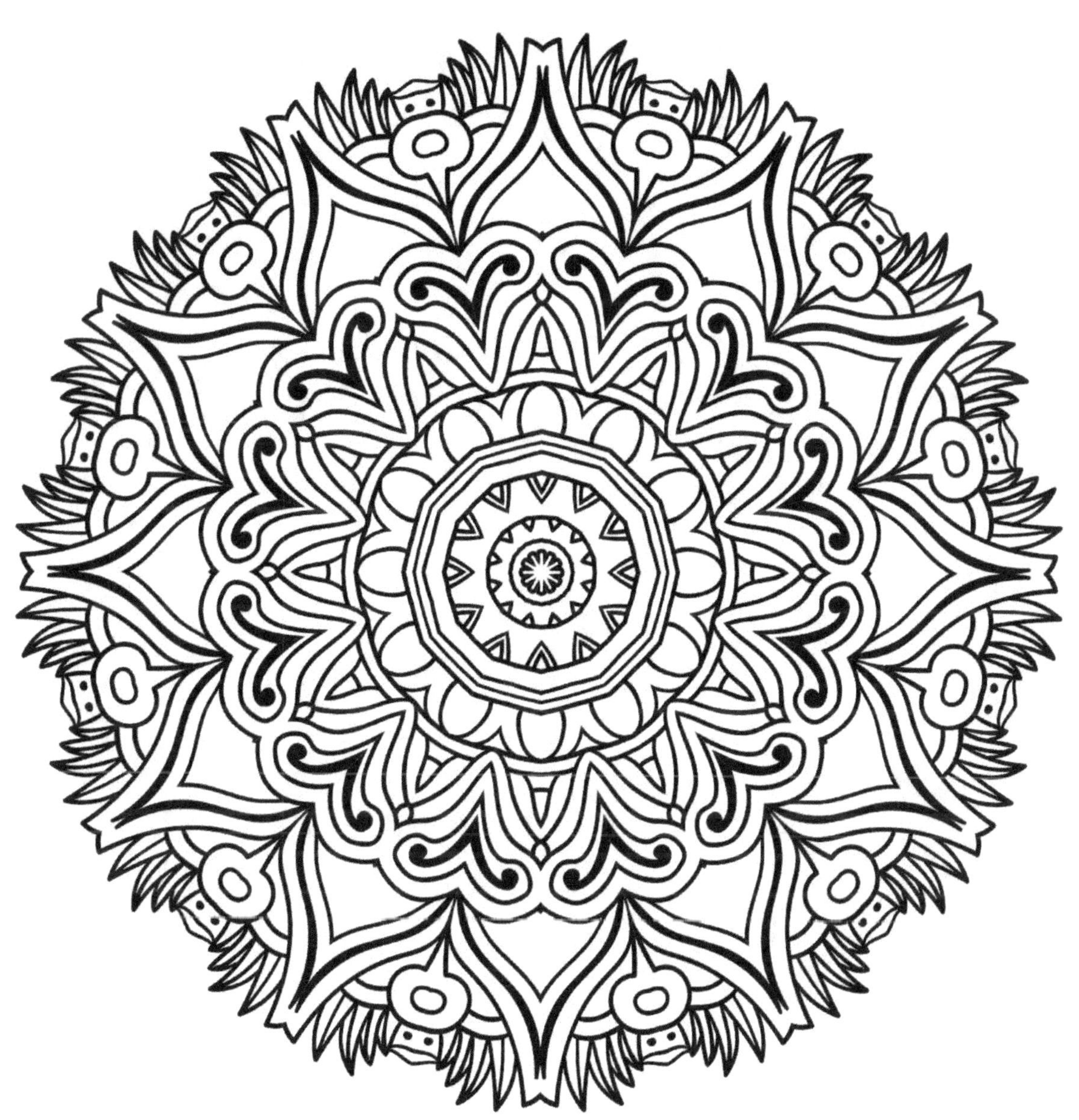

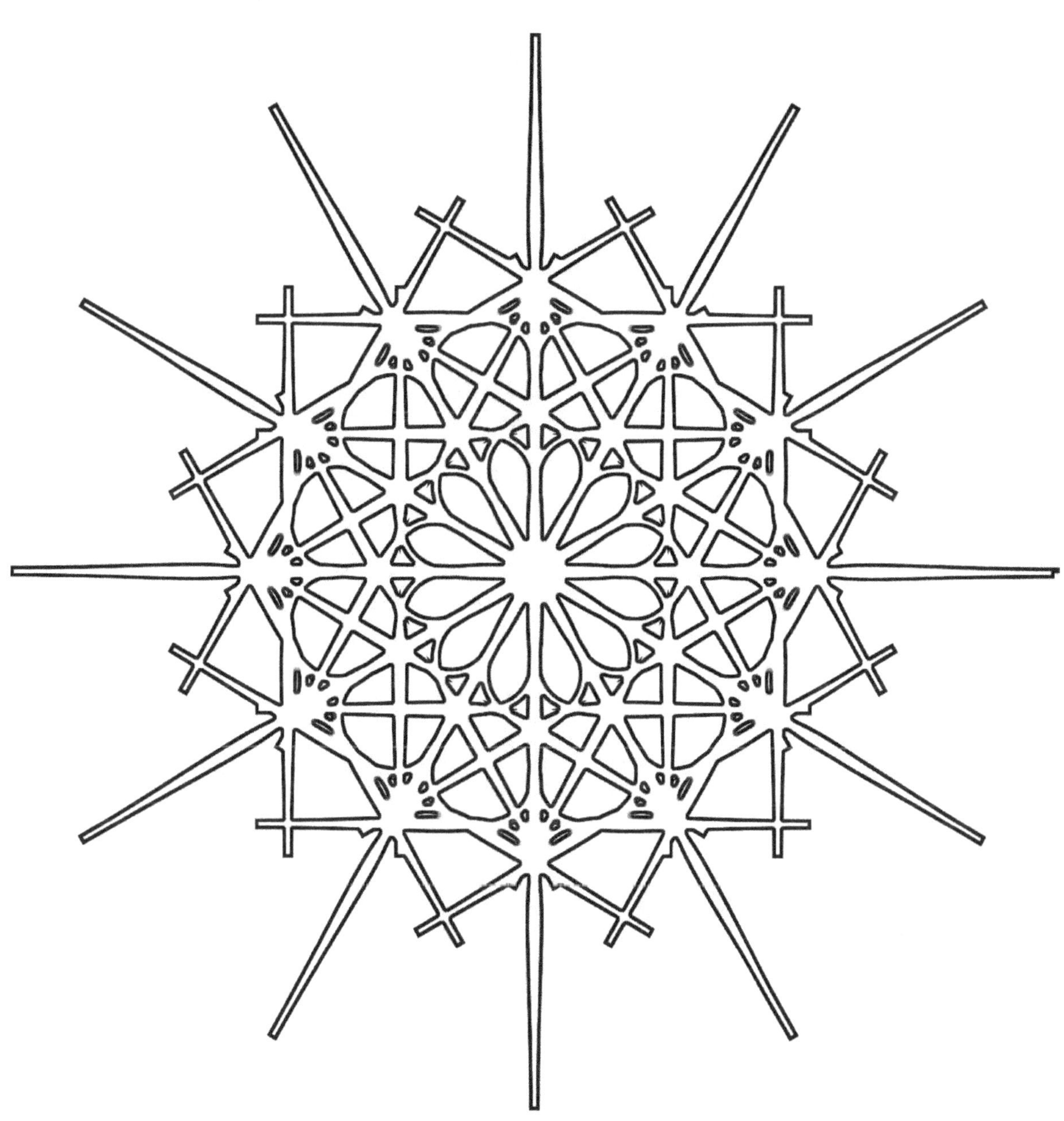

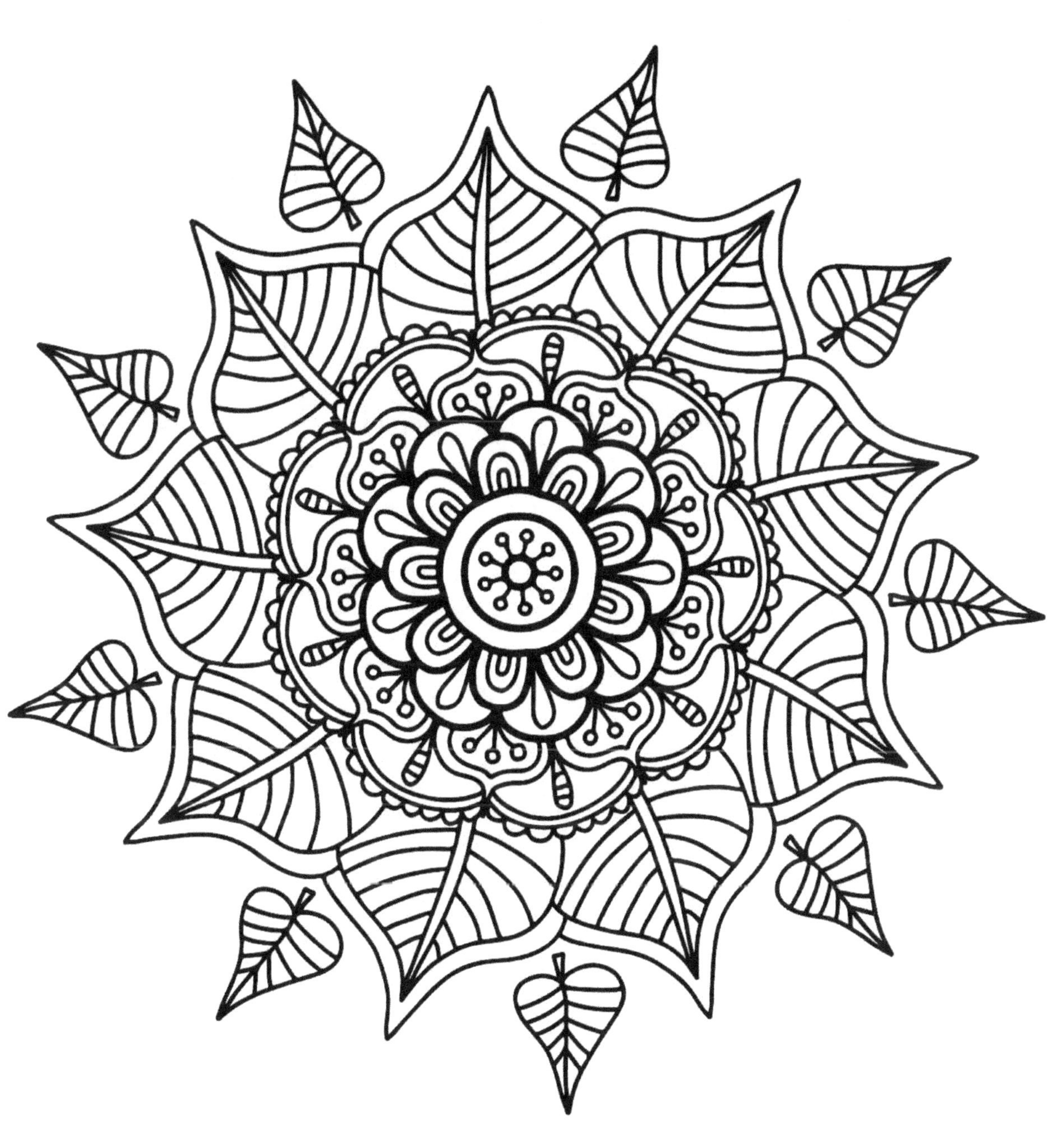

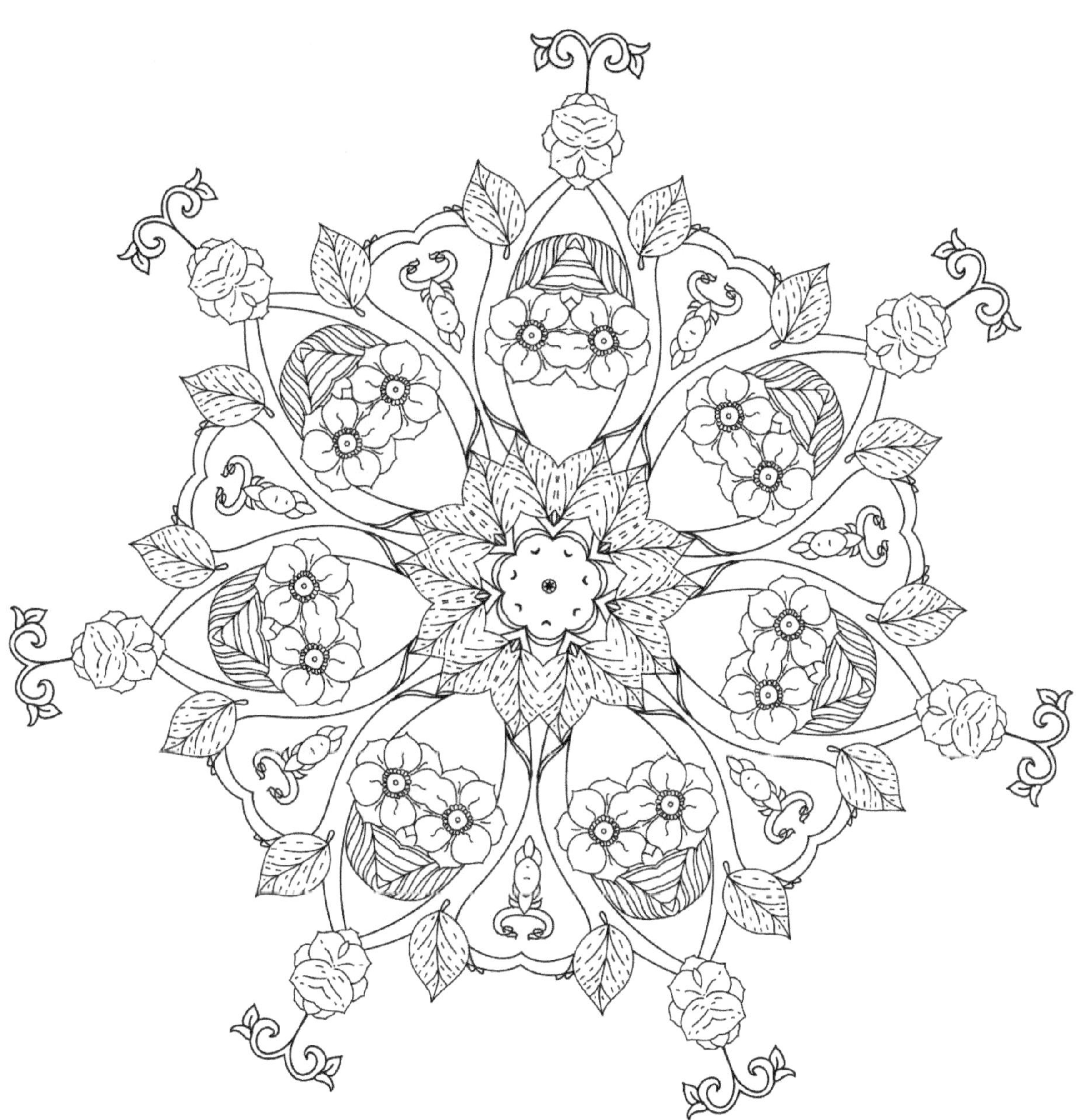

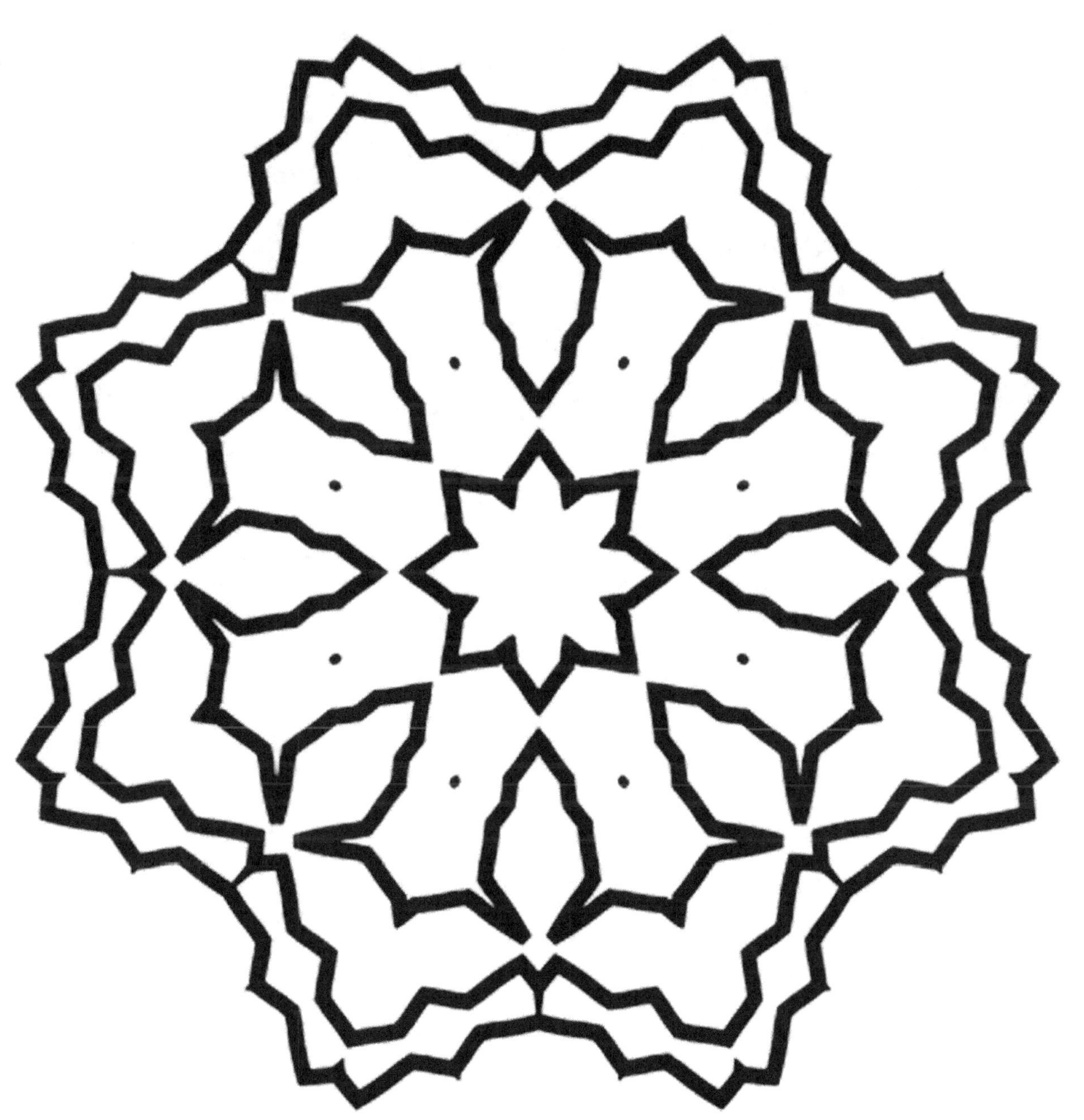

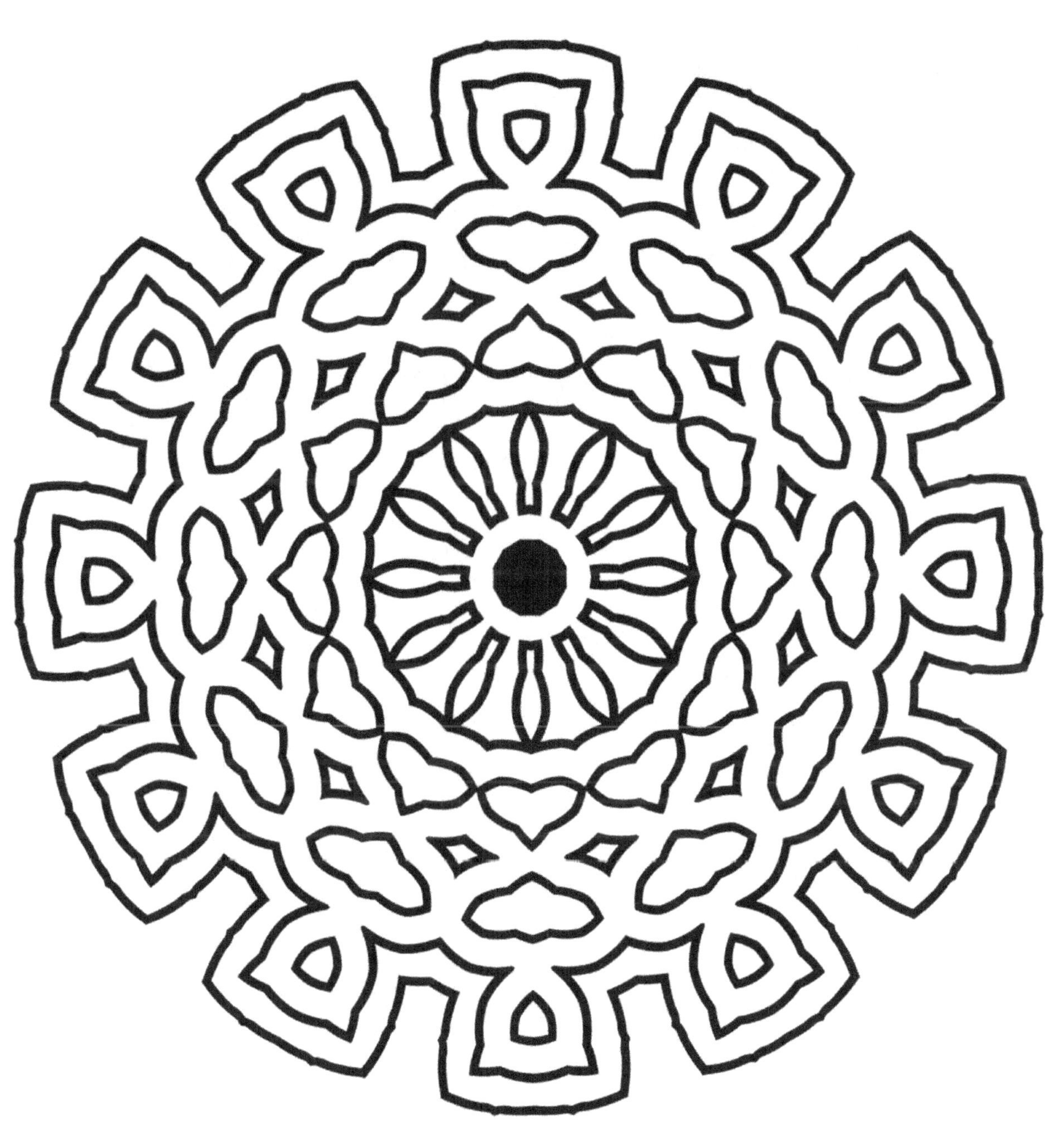

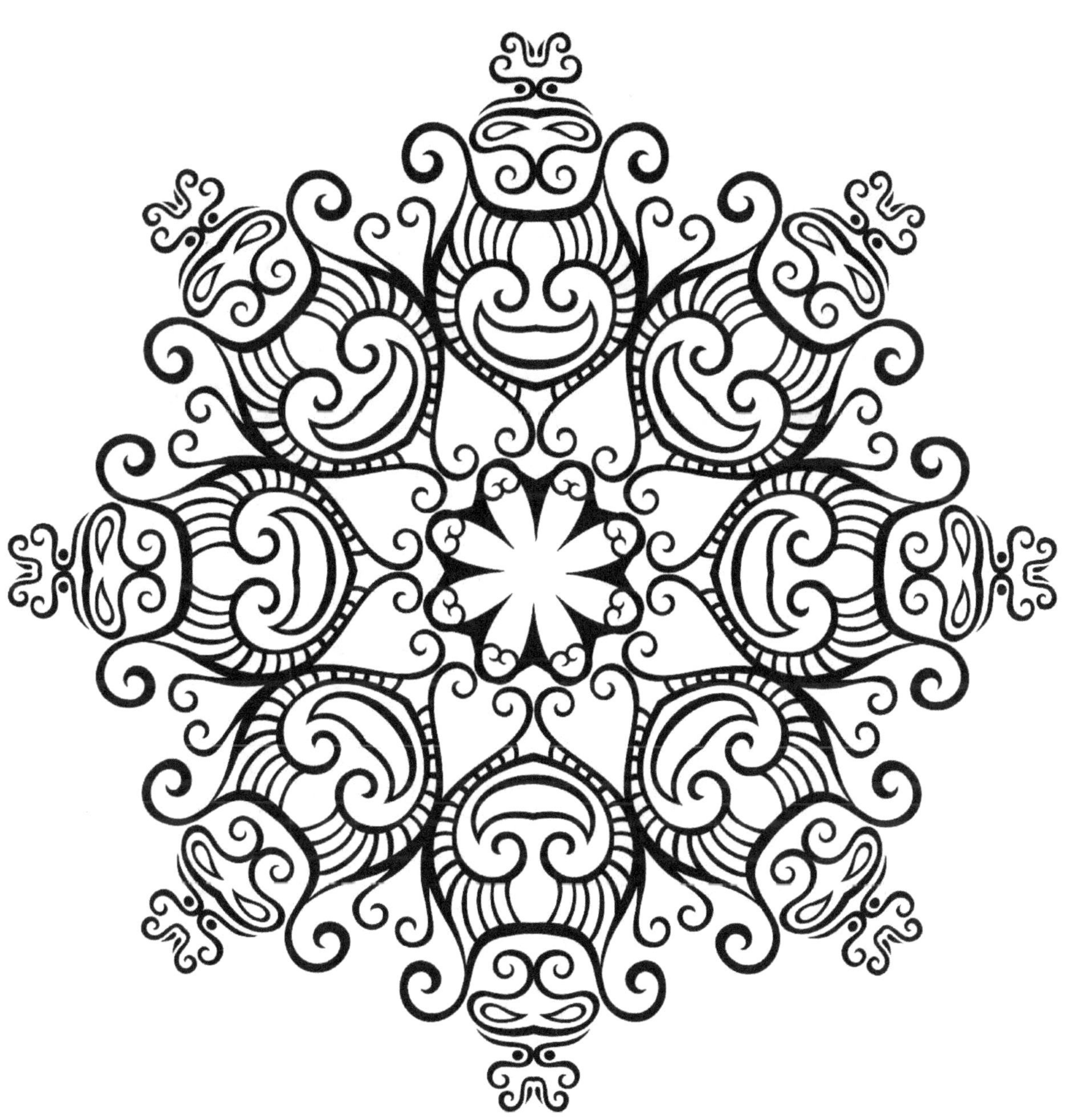

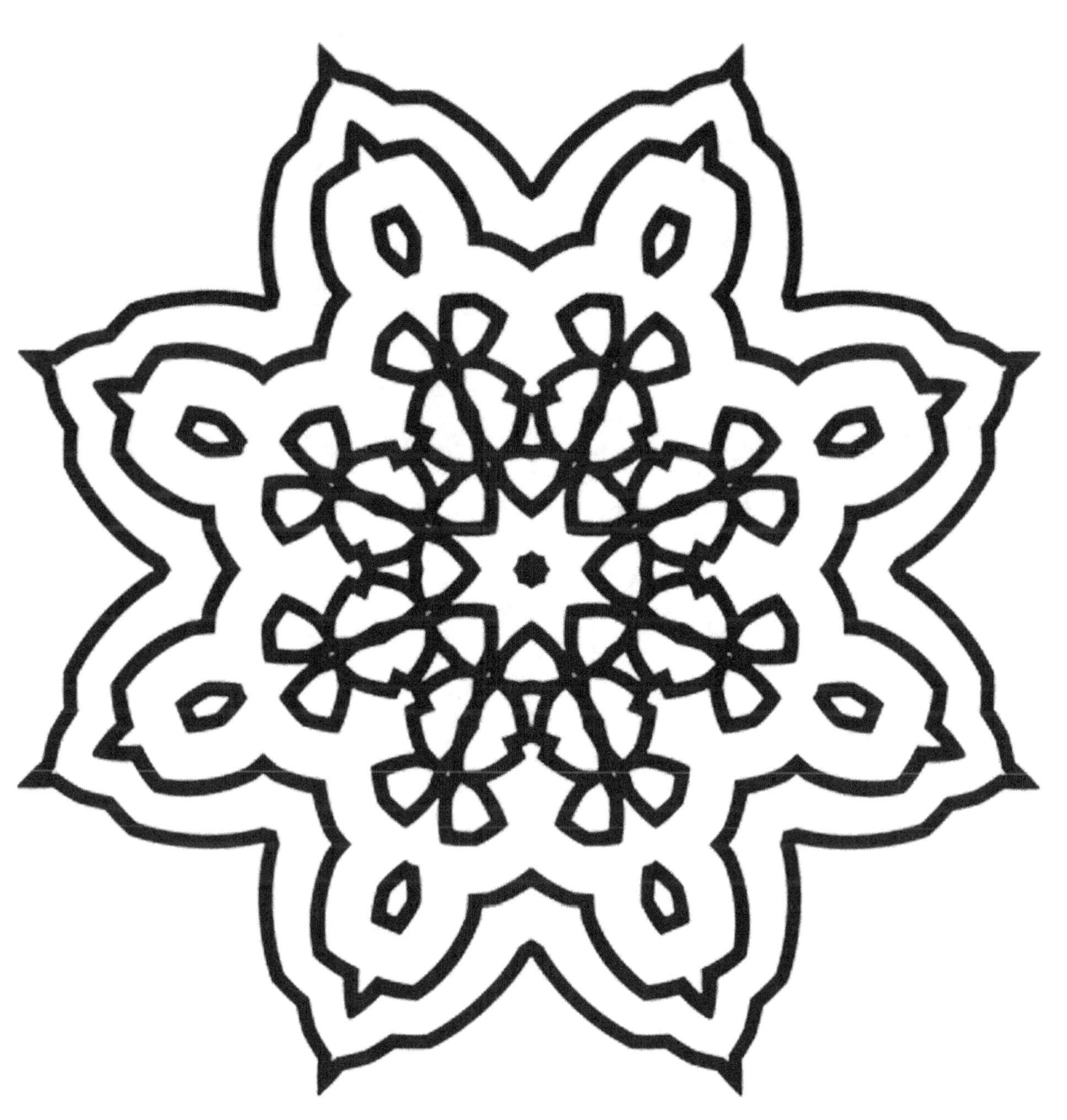

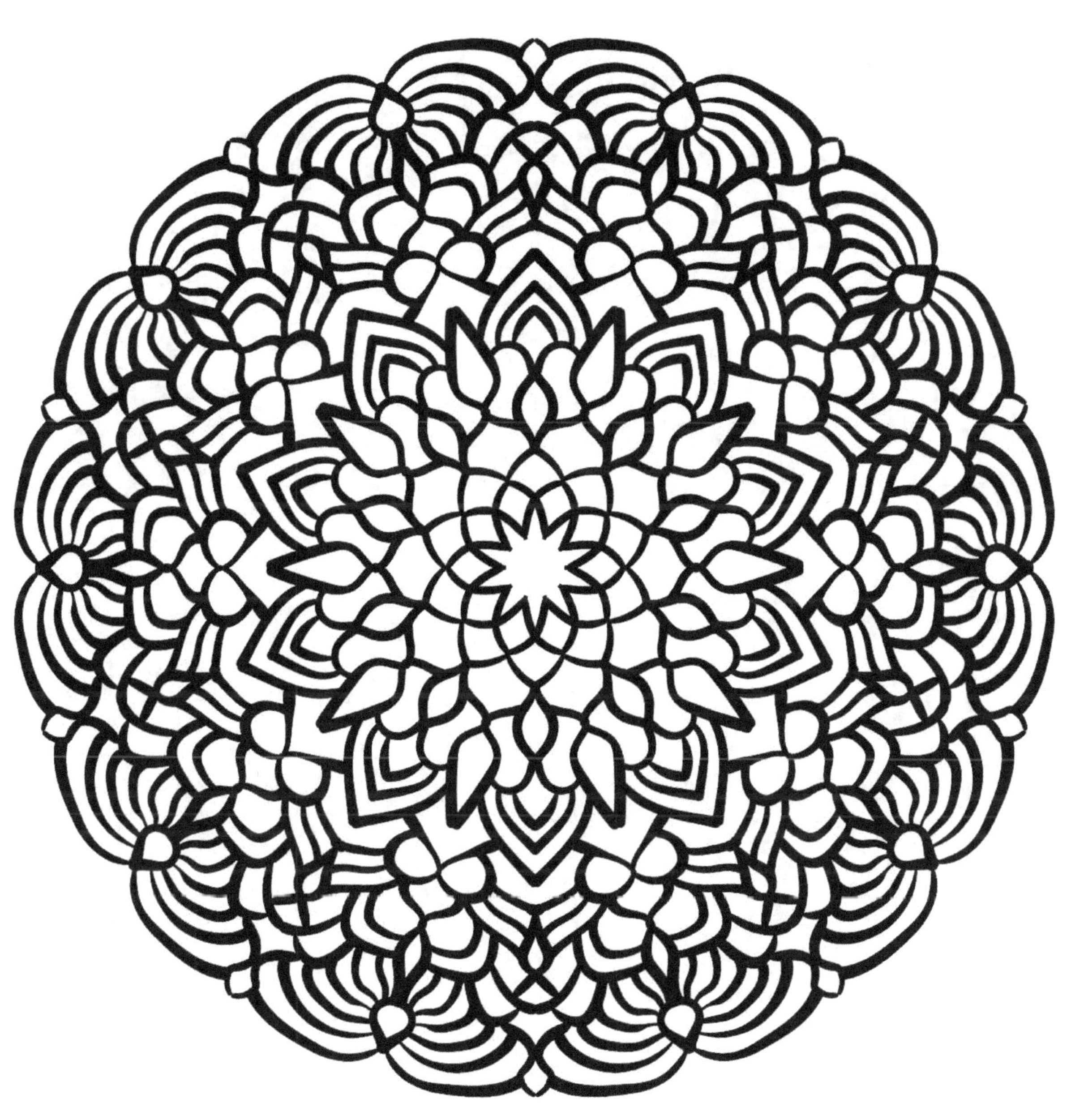

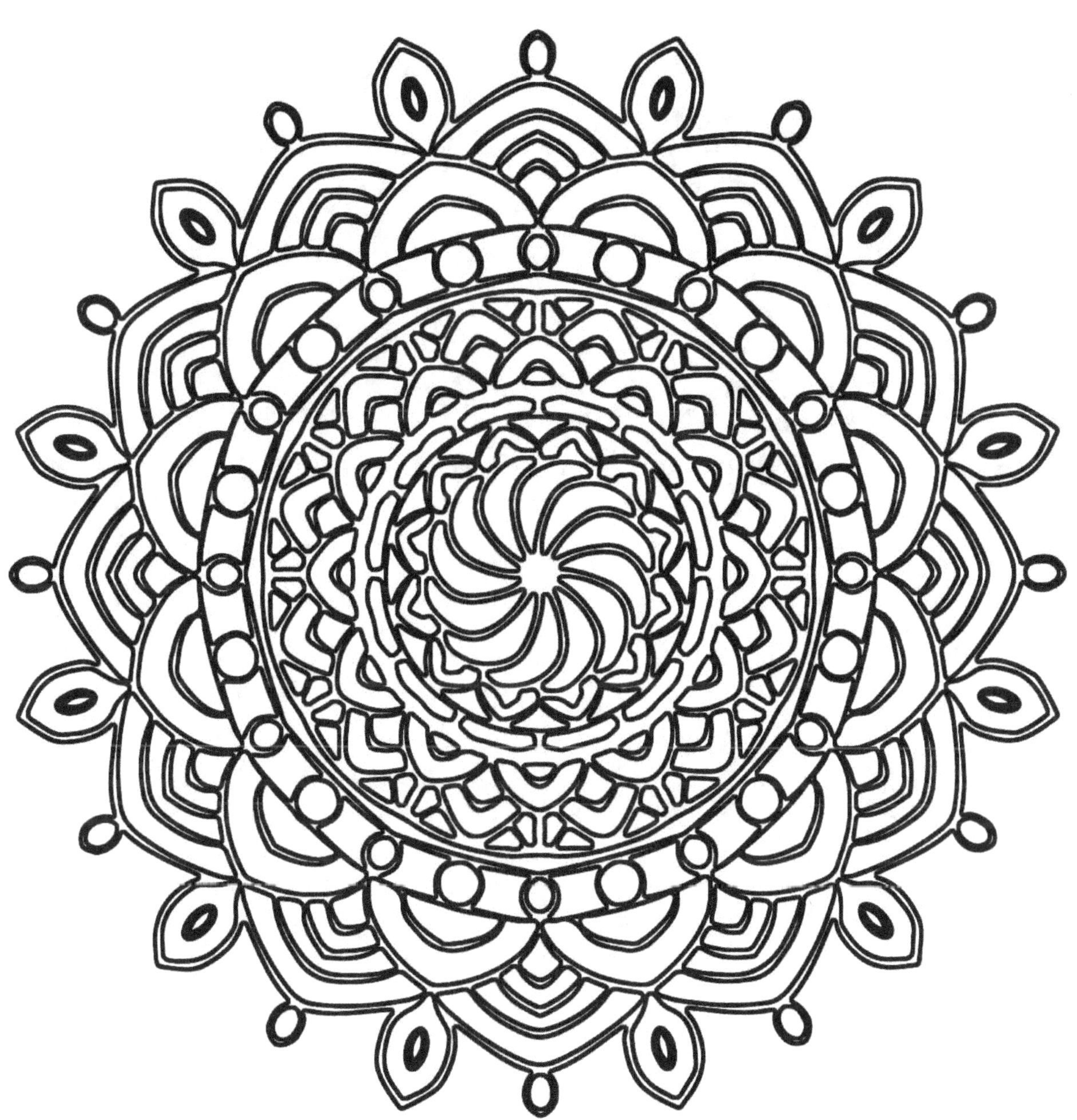